W9-AWS-695

THIS QUEST BELONGS TO

_____

NAME

THE JOURNEY BEGINS

_____

DATE

JOHN MACARTHUR

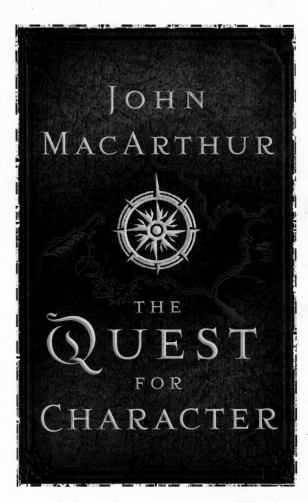

THE QUEST FOR CHARACTER

COUNTRYMAN

NASHVILLE, TENNESSEE

Copyright © 2006 by John MacArthur.

Published by J. Countryman®, a division of Thomas Nelson Inc.,
Nashville, Tennessee 37214

All rights reserved. No portion of this publication may be reproduced,
stored in a retrieval system or transmitted in any form by any means—
except for brief quotations in printed reviews—without the prior written
permission of the publisher.

J. Countryman® is a trademark of Thomas Nelson, Inc.

All Scripture quotations in this book, except those noted otherwise,
are from the *New King James Version* (NKJV) ©1979, 1980, 1982, 1992,
Thomas Nelson, Inc., Publisher. Used by permission.
Quotations marked NASB are from the *New American Standard Bible,*
© 1960, 1962, 1963, 1968, 1971, 1972, 1973, 1975, 1977, 1988, and 1995
by The Lockman Foundation, and are used by permission.
Quotations marked KJV are from the *King James Version* of the Bible.

Edited by Phillip R. Johnson

Design: Lookout Design | Stillwater, Minnesota

ISBN 1 4041 0049 0

Printed and bound in Belgium

www.thomasnelson.com | www.jcountryman.com

www.gty.org.

"You will **seek** Me and *find* Me, when you **search** for Me with *all your heart.*"

—JEREMIAH 29:13

CONTENTS

THE CHARACTER CRISIS

Character. It has an old—fashioned sound to it, like a faded relic of the Victorian era. We live in a materialistic culture where prestige, prosperity, and popularity are valued more than genuine integrity. In fact, personal character hardly seems to matter very much at all nowadays—at least in the realms of mass media, entertainment, politics, and pop culture.

Only a few select moral qualities are still prized by society at large. They are chiefly liberal community values such as diversity, tolerance, and broad—mindedness. Sometimes they are even called virtues. But when traits like those are blended with hypocrisy or employed to justify some other iniquity, they become mere caricatures of authentic virtue.

Meanwhile, genuine individual virtue—the stuff of which true, timeless, praiseworthy character is made—has been formally relegated to the sphere of "personal" things best not talked about openly. These days, even an elected national leader's personal character is supposed to be treated as a wholly private matter.

As a result, our society's most prominent celebrities include countless people who actually are known best for gigantic character flaws. Notice, for example, the people who usually grace the covers of celebrity magazines. Very few are decent role models. Often they are actually people who exemplify the worst kinds of character traits. No morally sane, thinking parents would ever hope for their own children to emulate the lifestyles or embrace the values of most of our society's best–known figures. Big personalities are highly revered anyway, because celebrity itself counts more than character in a society without any moral anchor.

> PEOPLE TODAY LITERALLY ENTERTAIN THEMSELVES WITH INIQUITY. . . . VIRTUE AND INFAMY HAVE TRADED PLACES.

In fact, over the past few decades so many famous people in our society have been charged with serious crimes that a cable television series is devoted exclusively to covering stories about the legal problems of some of our culture's favorite figures. Still, both the public and the media continue to confer celebrity status on more and more bizarre characters.

How have we come to this? The greatest cultures throughout human history have always reserved the highest positions of eminence and respect for true heroes—people who distinguish themselves by self–sacrifice, moral excellence, or some truly great accomplishment. The only societies that confer celebrity status on immoral and villainous people have been cultures in serious decline and on the precipice of utter ruin.

One of the universally understood rules of thumb that governed western society until a few short decades ago was that people who achieved fame had a duty to be wholesome role models. Even men and women who weren't really of sterling virtue in private sought to keep their character flaws hidden from the public—because if their moral defects became known, they lost their star status. Political figures could not remain in office if they were found culpable for any scandalous moral indiscretion.

That is no longer the case. Today's celebrities proudly flaunt their decadence. With the rise of a massive entertainment industry in the second half of the twentieth century, celebrity became a cheap and shallow commodity.

HONEST CHARACTER IS NOW SEEN AS TOTALLY OPTIONAL—OR WORSE, HOPELESSLY UNFASHIONABLE.

Honest character is now seen as totally optional—or worse, hopelessly unfashionable. As a matter of fact, in certain segments of today's entertainment and music industries, authentic virtue would be practically incompatible with fame and success. Some of the best-known figures in the recording industry, for example, are avowed gangsters who openly glorify evil in their lyrics. It is frightening to contemplate the future of a society where so many people so badly lacking in character can attain celebrity status so easily—and often hang onto their fame and influence no matter what crimes they commit.

The Bible says that is exactly what happens when a society rejects God and thereby incurs His righteous judgment. Romans 1:21–32 describes the downward path of a culture abandoned to sin. Take note of the roster of evils that finally overwhelm every fallen society. The list closely resembles everything currently fashionable in the world of entertainment and celebrity:

> *Even as they did not like to retain God in their knowledge, God gave them over to a debased mind, to do those things which are not fitting; being filled with all unrighteousness, sexual immorality, wickedness, covetousness, maliciousness; full of envy, murder, strife, deceit, evil–mindedness; they are whisperers, backbiters, haters of God, violent, proud, boasters, inventors of evil things, disobedient to parents, undiscerning, untrustworthy, unloving, unforgiving, unmerciful; who, knowing the righteous judgment of God, that those who practice such things are deserving of death, not only do the same but also approve of those who practice them.*

—ROMANS 1:28–32

That describes our culture to the letter, doesn't it? People today literally entertain themselves with iniquity, heedlessly applauding those who sin most flagrantly. Society today makes celebrities of people who in our grandparents' generation would have been deemed the most contemptible rogues. Almost everything that used to be considered shameful is now celebrated. We therefore live in a culture where personal character and individual virtue are rapidly evaporating at almost every level. Virtue and infamy have traded places.

According to the Bible, God designed us to be men and women of exemplary character. He repeatedly commands us to pursue what is virtuous and shun what is evil. From cover to cover in Scripture, iniquity is condemned and virtue is exalted.

> TRULY EXCELLENT CHARACTER IS ACTUALLY A REFLECTION OF THE MORAL NATURE OF GOD HIMSELF. FOR THAT REASON, ALL THE VIRTUES ARE INTERDEPENDENT AND CLOSELY RELATED. AND ALL OF THEM ARE THE FRUIT OF GOD'S GRACE.

Clearly, we are supposed to be men and women of excellent character. We're commanded to "hold fast what is good [and] abstain from every form of evil" (1 Thessalonians 5:21–22).

But where do we go to learn how to do that? Popular culture will not point the way for us. Scripture alone is a reliable lamp for our feet and light for our path (Psalm 119:105). God's Word points the way plainly in the quest for character.

The Bible contains numerous lists of positive character qualities. Second Peter 1:5–8, for example, gives a catalogue of virtues and urges us to add to our faith. The fruit of the Spirit in Galatians 5, the qualities of authentic love in 1 Corinthians 13, and the Beatitudes in Matthew 5 all list similar traits that describe true excellence of character.

In our quest, we'll work through the biblical inventory of character traits outlined in those particular passages—and we'll look at them with an eye to personal and practical application. There will be some overlap and repetition, because true character is not merely the sum of several disconnected characteristics. Truly excellent character is actually a reflection of the moral nature of God Himself. For that reason, all virtues are inter-dependent and closely related. And all of them are the fruit of God's grace.

I hope you'll find this brief study both interesting and personally edifying. May you perceive the true beauty of Christ's character and desire to see it reproduced in your own life.

THE BEATITUDES

MATTHEW 5:3-12

Blessed are the poor in spirit,
   For theirs is the kingdom of heaven.
Blessed are those who mourn,
   For they shall be comforted.
Blessed are the meek,
   For they shall inherit the earth.
Blessed are those who hunger and
      thirst for righteousness,
   For they shall be filled.
Blessed are the merciful,
   For they shall obtain mercy
Blessed are the pure in heart,
   For they shall see God.
Blessed are the peacemakers,
   For they shall be called sons of God.
Blessed are those who are persecuted
      for righteousness' sake,
   For theirs is the kingdom of heaven.

A HUMBLE SPIRIT

The Beatitudes are among the most familiar texts of Scripture. They are the opening words of the Sermon on the Mount, and one of the key verses of the whole sermon is Matthew 5:48: "Therefore you shall be perfect, just as your Father in heaven is perfect."

The sermon exalts moral perfection, and it sets a standard so high that frankly no one on earth could ever even come close to the standard.

To make that point, Jesus used the Pharisees as examples. In one of the most startling statements in the whole Sermon on the Mount, He said, "I say to you, that unless your righteousness exceeds the righteousness of the scribes and Pharisees, you will by no means enter the kingdom of heaven" (Matthew 5:20).

> JESUS' SERMON . . . STARTS WITH A BLESSING FOR BROKEN PEOPLE WHO RECOGNIZE THEIR OWN SPIRITUAL BANKRUPTCY.

His audience must have gasped. The Pharisees were well known for their fastidious observance of the fine points of the Old Testament law. Just for good measure, they had added some extra rules of their own.

For example, they went through a series of elaborate ceremonial washings every time they ate. (In Matthew 15:1–2, they even challenged Jesus and His disciples because they did not follow that manmade rule.) They fasted regularly, prayed often and publicly, and wore special garments that supposedly signified their devotion to the law.

In the minds of Jesus' listeners, the Pharisees epitomized the highest level of personal righteousness it was possible to attain on earth.

Jesus must have stunned the whole crowd when He said all of that wasn't good enough.

But the Pharisees' approach to seeking God's approval was all wrong. They were trying to manufacture their own brand of righteousness. In other words, everything they did was tainted with *self–righteousness*. Instead of making them humble, their religion made them proud and haughty.

> WE ARE NOT FUNDAMENTALLY GOOD. WE ARE NOT IN ANY WAY SPIRITUALLY SELF–SUFFICIENT. WE ARE FALLEN SINNERS IN DESPERATE NEED OF A SAVIOR. WE ARE SPIRITUAL PAUPERS.

Jesus' sermon specifically condemned that kind of self–righteousness. He therefore starts with a blessing for broken people who recognize their own spiritual bankruptcy: *"Blessed are the poor in spirit"* (Matthew 15:3).

The virtue He is describing is true spiritual humility. It is a recognition that we have nothing whatsoever that would commend us to God. We are not spiritually affluent. We are not fundamentally good. We are not in any way spiritually self—sufficient. We are fallen sinners in desperate need of a Savior. We are spiritual paupers.

Genuine character starts with that realization. It's a hard and humbling truth to face squarely. But if you try to divorce even the finest of human traits from basic spiritual humility, all the actual virtue is gone. The trait becomes a form of self—righteousness.

If you don't sense your own spiritual poverty, I want to encourage you to meditate on the majesty of God's law and the reality that even one broken commandment would be enough to condemn a person. Scripture says, "Whoever shall keep the whole law, and yet stumble in one point, he is guilty of all" (James 2:10).

Contemplate that truth while realizing that every one of us has transgressed God's law not once but countless times, and you will begin to grasp why humility before God is the first and most essential of all virtues.

Our spiritual need is far greater than any of us truly realizes. But if you can begin to grasp the idea, it ought to impress on your heart a deep sense of spiritual poverty. At our very best, we are nothing more than spiritual beggars. And that, Jesus said, is the first step toward the kind of character God can bless.

Humility before God is the *first* and *most* *essential* of all virtues.

2

A REPENTANT SORROW

Jesus' second beatitude is often misunderstood: *"Blessed are those who mourn"* (Matthew 5:4). The context reveals that He is not speaking of the kind of mourning related to earthly bereavement; instead it's grieving over one's own guilt, the sorrow of repentance over sin.

This beatitude echoes a familiar Old Testament text, Isaiah 61:1–2, where Israel's Messiah speaks prophetically:

The Spirit of the Lord GOD is
    upon Me,
Because the LORD has
    anointed Me
To preach good tidings to
    the poor;
He has sent Me to heal the
    brokenhearted,
To proclaim liberty to the
    captives,
And the opening of the prison
    to those who are bound;
To proclaim the acceptable
    year of the LORD,

And the day of vengeance of
    our God;
To comfort all who mourn,
To console those who mourn
    in Zion,
To give them beauty for ashes,
The oil of joy for mourning,
The garment of praise for the
    spirit of heaviness;
That they may be called trees
    of righteousness,
The planting of the LORD, that
    He may be glorified.

Centuries later, Jesus read from this passage in the synagogue at Nazareth at the start of His public ministry (Luke 4:16–21). He declared that the prophecy's fulfillment was beginning that very day. So it's undeniably clear that this was a prophecy about Christ. It's fitting, then, that He borrowed its expressions for the opening words of his greatest sermon.

Isaiah's prophecy describes a time when God's people would turn from their sins and mourn over them. He would respond with spiritual renewal, comforting their mourning hearts, giving them joy in place of their sorrow, and freeing them from the bondage of their own sin.

In other words, this speaks of the mourning of repentance. This is another virtue that is incompatible with self–righteousness. In fact, it is simply another perspective on the same truth Jesus spoke of in the first beatitude. Realizing you are spiritually bankrupt is a truth you grasp

> REALIZING YOU ARE SPIRITUALLY BANKRUPT IS A TRUTH YOU GRASP INTELLECTUALLY. MOURNING OVER YOUR SIN IS THE NATURAL RESPONSE OF THE EMOTIONS.

intellectually. Mourning over your sin is the natural response of the emotions.

The apostle Paul spoke of this kind of sorrow: "Godly sorrow produces repentance leading to salvation, not to be regretted" (2 Corinthians 7:10). This kind of sorrow has a healing effect. It involves painful anguish over the wickedness of our own sin. But because it produces repentance, it results in forgiveness— and that is the only unregrettable answer to all our regrets.

There is, however, another kind of sorrow that is no virtue, and Paul speaks of it in the second half of that same verse: "But the sorrow of the world produces death." *Worldly* sorrow is characterized by resentment over our sin's *consequences*. Its ultimate fruit, the Bible says, is death.

CHRIST TOOK AWAY [PETER'S] SORROW AND COMFORTED HIM WITH FULL FORGIVENESS. THAT'S EXACTLY WHAT THIS BEATITUDE PROMISES.

Judas regretted what he did and killed himself for it. That's the sorrow that leads to death. Peter denied Christ the same night Judas betrayed Him, but Peter's shame and anguish brought him back to Christ for forgiveness and cleansing, which he received. Christ took away his sorrow and comforted him with full forgiveness. That's exactly what this beatitude promises. It's one of the fundamental features of truly godly character.

3

A MEEK COMPOSURE

"The meek . . . shall inherit the earth," Jesus said (Matthew 5:5). Those may be the most familiar and frequently quoted words in all the Beatitudes.

What kind of attitude was Jesus commending? What is *meekness*? Is it a milksop, fainthearted, spineless kind of timidity? Not at all. Moses was nothing like that, and Scripture says Moses was the meekest man on earth (Numbers 12:3). Clearly, meekness is not weakness.

As a matter of fact, meekness is *strength under control*. The idea is closely related to the expression "poor in spirit" in verse 3. Both expressions speak of humility. But

> MEEKNESS IS NOT
> WEAKNESS. . . .
> MEEKNESS IS STRENGTH
> UNDER CONTROL.

meekness is the aspect of humility that is manifest in a mild, longsuffering, patient disposition. Meekness is often characterized as the polar opposite of an angry personality, and I think that gets close to the truth.

I like to look at it this way: brokenness of spirit (v. 3) is humility that arises from the knowledge that I am sinful.

Meekness (v. 5) is humility that arises from the knowledge that God is holy.

Meekness was not highly prized in the culture of first—century Galilee, where Jesus preached this sermon. The Roman city of Tiberias was a short walk away from this location. It was a resort town built for the self—indulgent Roman authorities, who equated meekness with weakness.

On the other hand, Galilean society itself did not esteem meekness very highly. Galilee was a hotbed of Jewish insurgency against Roman rule. Luke 13:1 mentions some Galilean Zealots who were brutally slain by Pontius Pilate at the altar in Jerusalem. The Zealots were a sect of violent political insurrectionists who represented a strain of thought in Galilean life that despised meekness as much as the haughty Romans did.

> MEEKNESS . . . IS WHERE HUMILITY AND SELF—CONTROL MEET.

Furthermore, Jewish religion in that era was strongly influenced by the Pharisees' teaching. Their example often fostered pride, self—sufficiency, hypocritical piousness, arrogance, and self—righteousness. All of that was incompatible with the notion of meekness.

Most of the people in Galilee and Judea were anticipating a Messiah who would come as a conquering hero—a military leader who would unite Israel against her enemies, sweep them away, and finally usher in the kingdom of God on earth.

But Jesus was meek. He "did not come to destroy men's lives but to save them" (Luke 9:56). When He formally entered

Jerusalem as king, it was not on a stallion decked out for battle. He was riding on the foal of a donkey (Matthew 21:5). He came with the express purpose of dying, not subduing others by force.

And He thus left us an example to follow: "Who committed no sin, nor was deceit found in His mouth; who, when He was reviled, did not revile in return; when He suffered, He did not threaten, but committed Himself to Him who judges righteously" (1 Peter 2:22-23). That's the epitome of true meekness.

Jesus said such a one will inherit the earth. Not the mighty, vengeful, self–sufficient warrior type, but the meek person.

What does it mean to inherit the earth? For one thing, that's a promise of salvation and eternal life. It echoes the promise of Psalm 149:4: "He will beautify the [meek] with salvation." He will give them the world and eternal life, too.

Meekness, to sum up, is where humility and self–control meet. It's one of the most attractive and indispensable aspects of truly Christlike character. It's the one quality most necessary to tame an out–of–control ego, and as arrogance gives way to meekness, it is the cure for countless ills that often hinder the quest for character.

4

A PARCHED SOUL

The thread of promise that runs through all the Beatitudes is *happiness*. Don't imagine that real happiness is a giddy, whimsical attitude of hilarity. It's a deep and abiding sense of well-being, joy, and satisfaction. *True* happiness. *Real* fulfillment.

That's what the word "blessed" signifies. In other words, the Beatitudes are not merely the first signposts on our quest for character; they are also the keys to true happiness.

It makes for an interesting string of paradoxes. These are not truths the fallen human mind would ever be able to discover by any process of mere logic. Happiness is found in brokenness. Happiness is found in sorrow. Happiness is found in meekness. Happiness is found in hunger and thirst.

But the fourth beatitude explains how the deepest kind of satisfaction may yet be found in this fallen and usually unsatisfying world: *"Blessed are those who hunger and thirst for righteousness, for they shall be filled"* (Matthew 5:6).

Want to be truly satisfied? Cultivate and feed an appetite for righteousness.

Here is a genuine mark of authentic character. The average person craves things like pleasure, prestige, power, popularity, possessions, and other self—aggrandizing things. The person who has true character feeds a different set of appetites. He longs most of all for righteousness—the glory of God, the truth of Scripture, the fellowship of godly people, and Christlike virtue.

This beatitude is a perfect complement to the first one. Poverty of spirit and a parched soul longing for righteousness go hand in hand.

On the other hand, a love for values that are cheap, shallow, worldly, fleshly, or evil is incompatible with the true love of righteousness. "Do you not know that friendship with the world is enmity with God? Whoever therefore wants to be a friend of the world makes himself an enemy of God" (James 4:4).

> THE BEATITUDES ARE NOT MERELY THE FIRST SIGNPOSTS ON OUR QUEST FOR CHARACTER; THEY ARE ALSO THE KEYS TO TRUE HAPPINESS.

If your heart is dead and spiritually lifeless, you cannot by a sheer act of human will summon an appetite for true righteousness. Scripture says, "the carnal mind is enmity against God; for it is not subject to the law of God, nor indeed can be. So then, those who are in the flesh cannot please God" (Romans 8:7–8).

Not only that, every person is born into a state of spiritual death. We are fallen, sinful creatures—children of wrath.

That's why Jesus taught that we must be born again. "Most assuredly, I say to you, unless one is born again, he cannot see the kingdom of God" (John 3:3). What each person needs is new life. Ezekiel 36:26 portrays it as the implantation of a new heart to replace the stony dead one. With that new heart comes a new appetite for righteousness. Nurture and feed that appetite, and you will be satisfied.

If you are reading this and have never been born again, I am certain God has brought you to this point and shown you this truth for a reason. Only He can give you new life, a new heart, and a true hunger and thirst for righteousness. But Scripture makes this blessed promise: "Whoever calls on the name of the LORD shall be saved" (Romans 10:13). If you recognize your spiritual poverty, then turn to Christ as Lord and Savior. Ask Him to give you spiritual life by His Spirit. He promises He will turn no one away.

The great British Bible expositor D. Martyn Lloyd–Jones said this about the fourth beatitude: "If this verse is to you one of the most blessed statements of the whole of Scripture, you can be quite certain you are a Christian; if it is not, then you had better examine the foundations again".

Want to be truly satisfied?

Cultivate and feed an

appetite for righteousness.

If your heart is dead and

spiritually lifeless, you cannot by

a sheer act of human will summon

an appetite for true righteousness.

Turn to Christ as Lord and Savior.

Ask Him to give you spiritual life

by His Spirit. He promises He will

turn no one away.

5

A MERCIFUL
COMPASSION

Notice how every one of the Beatitudes focuses on what *we are*, not merely what we do. Jesus was not encouraging His hearers to act humble, put on a show of repentance, feign a spirit of meekness, or otherwise pretend to be righteous. That's where the Pharisees excelled. Jesus said they were like whitewashed tombs, sparkling clean and neat—looking on the outside, but full of death and decay on the inside (Matthew 23:27).

> EVERY ONE OF THE
> BEATITUDES FOCUSES
> ON WHAT WE *are*, NOT
> MERELY WHAT WE DO.

Genuine character is all about who we really are inside. It's not about what we look like to others. Character is not a facade or a veneer. If it's not real, then by definition it has nothing to do with *character*.

So when Jesus says, *"Blessed are the merciful, for they shall obtain mercy"* (Matthew 5:7), He is still speaking of an inward attitude, not just how we act. To be sure, if the attitude of mercy is real it will be manifest in merciful words and actions, too, "for out of the abundance of the heart the mouth speaks" (Matthew 12:34). And "as he thinks in his heart, so is he" (Proverbs 23:7).

There's a natural progression in the Beatitudes. Each quality of godly character leads naturally to the next. They all round out and perfect one another. This beatitude about mercy illustrates how that works: the person who recognizes he is merely a spiritual beggar will be more merciful toward others. Those who mourn over their sin will also show mercy to other sinners. Meekness is one of the qualities of mercy itself. And since mercy is an aspect of righteousness, those who hunger and thirst for righteousness will by definition be people who love mercy. So all the Beatitudes go hand in hand. It's impossible to manifest one in isolation from the others. As you cultivate one aspect of truly Christlike character, the others naturally develop with it.

Mercy is one of the great virtues that stems from the heart of God Himself. The Bible says, "The Lord is good to all, and His tender mercies are over all His works" (Psalm 145:9). His mercy is an inexhaustible resource, and it's the very reason we don't suffer instant destruction the moment we sin. "Through the Lord's mercies we are not consumed, because His compassions fail not. They are new every morning; great is Your faithfulness" (Lamentations 3:22–23).

Mercy is vital to godly character. If you want to reflect the epitome of God's own heart and character, cultivate mercy.

In fact, this is one of our primary duties: "He has shown you, O man, what is good; and what does the Lord require of you but to do justly, to love mercy, and to walk humbly with your God?" (Micah 6:8). In this beatitude, Jesus blesses a heart that loves mercy. Again, it is a character quality, but it never stops there. It is manifest in acts of goodness toward others.

Jesus said we should extend mercy even to our enemies: "I say to you, love your enemies, bless those who curse you, do good to those who hate you, and pray for those who spitefully use you and persecute you, that you may be sons of your Father in heaven; for He makes His sun rise on the evil and on the good, and sends rain on the just and on the unjust" (Matthew 5:44-45).

In other words, mercy colors God's dealings even with those who hate Him, and if our character is going to be a reflection of His, we must be merciful even to those who hate us. That's not a natural quality for fallen human hearts, but it is essential to the quest for authentic godly character.

All the Beatitudes go

hand in hand . . .

As you *cultivate* one

aspect of truly *Christlike*

character, the

others *naturally*

develop with it.

6

A PURE HEART

The sixth beatitude is a blessing for those who are holy:
"Blessed are the pure in heart, for they shall see God" (Matthew 5:8).
This statement seems to rise above the other Beatitudes and
summarize the truth contained in all of them. Indeed, it might be
seen as a summary statement of the whole Sermon on the Mount.

It's a call for clean and holy hearts. It speaks to the very point
on which most of the Pharisees' religion foundered. It sweeps
away all pretense and hypocrisy and teaches us that what really
counts in God's estimation is
the state of our hearts.

WHAT REALLY COUNTS IN
GOD'S ESTIMATION IS THE
STATE OF OUR HEARTS.

In that sense, it is a sobering
and daunting requirement.

No one can see God without a
pure heart. This is the same truth stated in different words by
Hebrews 12:14: "Pursue . . . holiness, without which no one
will see the Lord."

The problem is that none of us has a truly pure heart. Sin
tarnishes our whole being. That's what makes the quest for
character so difficult. And there's nothing we can do for ourselves
to make our hearts clean. That's the point of Proverbs 20:9:

"Who can say, 'I have made my heart clean, I am pure from my sin'?"

That brings up a vital truth. The Beatitudes, just like the Ten Commandments, condemn us all. But they serve a vital and very helpful purpose. They show us our need for a Savior and direct us to Christ for the forgiveness and cleansing we need.

Our sin is profound and abundant. We can't afford to pay its penalty, and we cannot free ourselves from its bondage.

That's why Christ died on behalf of sinners—to redeem us from that bondage. Throughout His life, He remained perfectly righteous, free from any guilt whatsoever. He alone had the purest of pure hearts. Scripture says He "committed no sin, nor was deceit found in His mouth" (1 Peter 2:22). He is "holy, harmless, undefiled, separate from sinners" (Hebrews 7:26). Yet in dying, He suffered divine retribution for all who trust Him. "He has borne our griefs and carried our sorrows. . . . He was wounded for our transgressions, He was bruised for our iniquities; the chastisement for our peace was upon Him" (Isaiah 53:4–5).

> THE BEATITUDES . . . CONDEMN US ALL. BUT THEY SERVE A VITAL AND VERY HELPFUL PURPOSE. THEY SHOW US OUR NEED FOR A SAVIOR.

Because He paid for sin in full, Scripture says, "If we confess our sins, He is faithful and just to forgive us our sins and to cleanse us from all unrighteousness" (1 John 1:9). Notice: the forgiveness He provides is not merely an act of mercy. It is also an act of justice because He has paid the penalty in full. And

We are *cleansed* and *fully* *forgiven* the moment we *first* trust Him with *authentic faith.*

therefore He can cleanse us from our unrighteousness and cleanse our impure hearts.

That does not speak of a one–time cleansing only. We are cleansed and fully forgiven the moment we first trust Him with authentic faith. Scripture refers to that as justification, which involves not just the forgiveness of our sin and the erasure of our guilt but also the imputation of Christ's righteousness to us. Just as He took our guilt and paid for it, He puts His righteousness on our account, and we get full credit for it.

> IN THE INTEGRITY OF A PERFECTLY PURE HEART, WE WILL SEE GOD.

But there is an ongoing cleansing that takes place daily as we continue confessing our sins and receiving His forgiveness. The Spirit of God conforms us to Christ's true likeness. That is how true Christlike character becomes ours.

David understood this process. When he sinned—even when he sinned monstrously—he prayed, "Create in me a clean heart, O God, and renew a steadfast spirit within me" (Psalm 51:10).

That ought to be the daily prayer of every truly upright soul. We don't have completely pure hearts yet. Daily we are being conformed to the image of Christ, and one day He will glorify us completely (1 John 3:2), so that in the integrity of a perfectly pure heart, we will see God.

7

A PASSION FOR PEACE

"Blessed are the peacemakers, for they shall be called sons of God" (Matthew 5:9). Here is another crucial attribute of godly character: a love for peace.

Scripture refers to God as "the God of peace" (Philippians 4:9). Creation itself perfectly manifests that aspect of God's nature. Eden was created to be a peaceful paradise for humanity. But Adam forfeited the harmony of Eden when he sinned. His sin was like a declaration of war against God's right to rule His own creation. It therefore broke the peace of Eden.

> [ADAM'S] SIN WAS LIKE A DECLARATION OF WAR AGAINST GOD'S RIGHT TO RULE HIS OWN CREATION.

Adam's rebellion against God had disastrous long–range effects. It set the entire human race at enmity with God. All the evils that disrupt the peacefulness of our earthly existence stem from the curse of sin that began with Adam. Redemptive history is the long saga of how God Himself intervenes to save the human race from its own sin, overthrow evil, and restore peace to His creation.

At the end of history, when Christ establishes His rightful kingdom, peace will once again reign, even here on earth.

Meanwhile, we are to be lovers of peace. That doesn't mean we will never have any conflict, or even that we should try to avoid conflicts at any cost. As a matter of fact, the Bible portrays the Christian life as a perpetual state of warfare (Ephesians 6:12–20). Even the final beatitude reminds us that persecution and conflict are inevitable realities for every Christian.

THE STARTING POINT FOR AUTHENTIC PEACE IS *PEACE WITH GOD*.

Still, we ought to love peace and hate conflict. We ought to be peaceable and not pugnacious. Christ, who encountered His share of conflict during His earthly ministry, never aroused conflict for conflict's sake.

On the other hand, Jesus never sought to avoid conflict or persecution for the sake of a false peace. Scripture says, "The wisdom that is from above is *first* pure, *then* peaceable" (James 3:17, emphasis added). As much as we love peace and prefer peace over any kind of conflict, making peace with evil is unthinkable. Sanctioning evil brings no true peace at all.

Holiness is, after all, an essential prerequisite for real peace. In the previous chapter, we considered a partial quotation from Hebrews 12:14. Here's the full verse: "Pursue peace with all people, and holiness, without which no one will see the Lord." Peace and holiness are indivisible partners. Try to divorce the two virtues and you destroy them both. The person who truly loves holiness will also love peace, and vice versa.

That means there ultimately can be no real peace for those who despise holiness. "'There is no peace,' says my God, 'for the wicked'" (Isaiah 57:21). Naturally, then, anyone who genuinely loves holiness will spurn the false, worldly "peace" of blithe tolerance for evil things. That is not true peace in any sense. It's actually a thin disguise for fallen humanity's hostility against God.

The starting point for authentic peace is *peace with God.* That's why Christ's primary earthly mission was to make peace with God on behalf of those who trust Him, and He accomplished that by removing our sins as a barrier to God's blessing. "Therefore, having been justified by faith, we have peace with God through our Lord Jesus Christ" (Romans 5:1).

One of the best ways we can be peacemakers is by proclaiming the gospel of reconciliation to a world in conflict. In the words of the apostle Paul, "we are ambassadors for Christ, as though God were pleading through us: we implore you on Christ's behalf, be reconciled to God" (2 Corinthians 5:20).

Redemptive *history* is the long saga of how God Himself *intervenes* *to save* the human race from its own sin, overthrow evil, and **restore peace** to His creation.

8

A STEADFAST LOVE FOR CHRIST

The longest of the Beatitudes is the final one: *"Blessed are those who are persecuted for righteousness' sake, for theirs is the kingdom of heaven. Blessed are you when they revile and persecute you, and say all kinds of evil against you falsely for My sake. Rejoice and be exceedingly glad, for great is your reward in heaven, for so they persecuted the prophets who were before you"* (Matthew 5:10–12).

> SCRIPTURE IS ABSOLUTELY CLEAR ABOUT THE INEVITABILITY OF PERSECUTION.

It's ironic and highly significant that Jesus moves immediately from the idea of encouraging peacemakers to the reality that a person with righteous character inevitably will incur persecution. In one sense people with godly character are peacemakers; in another sense, they are troublemakers.

Scripture is absolutely clear about the inevitability of persecution: "All who desire to live godly in Christ Jesus will suffer persecution" (2 Timothy 3:12).

Notice, however, that this is the only beatitude that comes with a double blessing. Jesus begins in verse 10 with the words

"Blessed are those . . . " Verse 11 repeats the same blessing, but in a more personal way: "Blessed are *you* . . . " These are wonderful words of comfort for anyone suffering persecution wrongfully. No matter how people revile and persecute you, Jesus' blessing abides on you when you suffer for His sake.

The persecution He describes is a specific kind. He's not blessing those who are merely suffering the due consequences of some sin. This is not a blessing for someone being hounded by bill collectors for overdue payments. It's not an expression of sympathy for everyone who is hassled by a harsh boss or a cantankerous neighbor. It's not a word of encouragement for those struggling with the everyday trials of life, like high gasoline prices or frustrating traffic jams.

This beatitude applies to those who take a stand for Christ and suffer because of it. What Jesus is talking about here is real persecution. There are two vital qualifying expressions: "*falsely*," and "*for My sake*."

First of all, let's be sure that all the evil things our tormenters say about us are undeserved and unprovoked. A televangelist who dishonors Christ through ungodly behavior cannot claim the blessing of the persecuted when the world scorns him for his hypocrisy. The street preacher with a bullhorn who deliberately says insulting things that provoke the wrath of passers—by cannot claim the comforts of this blessing. Unfortunately, many people do ungracious things in the name of Christ and then glory in the contempt that comes their way. That is not at all the attitude Jesus blesses in this text.

Don't take persecution as a personal insult, and don't retaliate in kind. But endure the affront for Jesus' sake, remembering His example.

Instead, He is blessing people who are innocently and falsely accused by others for no reason other than the persecutors' resentment of everything righteous. When you represent Christ in a Christlike way, it is inevitable that those who hate Him will make you the object of their mockery. Insults, lying accusations, and sometimes even worse kinds of abuse will be hurled at you. When that happens, don't be ashamed; don't abandon your testimony for Christ; but "rejoice and be exceedingly glad." You're in good company. Every prophet in history has been similarly abused.

Second, remember for whose sake you are suffering. Don't take persecution as a personal insult, and don't retaliate in kind. But endure the affront for Jesus' sake,

> THIS BEATITUDE APPLIES TO THOSE WHO TAKE A STAND FOR CHRIST AND SUFFER BECAUSE OF IT.

remembering His example of never returning reviling for reviling or threat for threat (1 Peter 2:23).

It's a mark of the highest, most honorable character if you can accept such abuse and remain steadfast and unmovable, knowing that your labor and your love for Christ are not in vain (1 Corinthians 15:58).

THE PROGRESS OF FAITH

2 PETER 1:5-8

Giving all diligence, add to your
faith virtue, to virtue knowledge,
to knowledge self—control,
to self—control perseverance,
to perseverance godliness,
to godliness brotherly kindness,
and to brotherly kindness love.
For if these things are yours and
abound, you will be neither barren
nor unfruitful in the knowledge
of our Lord Jesus Christ.

9

FAITH

The Beatitudes outline the essential characteristics of true faith. Because they describe the citizens of Christ's kingdom, and entry into the kingdom is through faith alone, the Beatitudes in effect show us what the nature of faith is and what the fruit of authentic faith looks like.

Faith is the most essential aspect of true character. In fact, it is the basic foundation of every other virtue. No wonder we often say the person who lacks character is *unfaithful*.

> FAITH IS THE MOST ESSENTIAL ASPECT OF TRUE CHARACTER. . . . IT IS THE BASIC FOUNDATION OF EVERY OTHER VIRTUE.

"Giving all diligence, add to your faith..." (2 Peter 1:5). If you want to cultivate the kind of character that pleases and honors God, faith is the primary and nonnegotiable prerequisite. Hebrews 11:6 says, "Without faith it is impossible to please Him, for he who comes to God must believe that He is, and that He is a rewarder of those who diligently seek Him." One of the earliest and most important biblical descriptions of the way sinners are justified before God

is found in Genesis 15:6: "[Abraham] believed in the LORD, and He accounted it to him for righteousness."

The apostle Paul quotes that verse in Romans 4:3 and Galatians 3:6. Both times he uses the verse to show that faith is the essential instrument by which sinful people can lay hold of God's forgiveness and blessing. It is the means through which perfect righteousness is "accounted" to them in the reckoning of God.

What is this righteousness that is "reckoned" to the faithful? Scripture says repeatedly that it is the perfect righteousness of God made possible by Christ (Romans 3:22; 2 Corinthians 5:21; Philippians 3:9). Our faith unites us with Christ in a spiritual union whereby His life counts as our life and His perfect, flawless righteousness accrues to our eternal benefit and blessing.

Just as Christ took the sins of His people and paid for our guilt in full, so the full merit of His righteousness is written to our account in the divine reckoning. In biblical terms, righteousness is *imputed* to them (Romans 4:22–24).

It's a perfect exchange of the sinner's guilt for Christ's righteousness. It's also a perfect spiritual union with Him, so that all who are united with Him by faith share in His life as well as His death (Romans 6:3–5). His death pays in full the penalty of our sin, and His life provides all the righteousness we need for a perfect standing before the judgment throne of God. That is what Paul describes in 2 Corinthians 5:21: "For He made Him who knew no sin to be sin for us, that we might become the righteousness of God in Him." In other words, on the cross God treated Christ as if He had committed all the sins of every person who would ever believe in Him, so that He could treat them as if they lived Christ's perfect life.

That is what Scripture refers to as *justification*. It explains how sinners are forgiven and accepted in the courtroom of God without any condemnation (Romans 8:1) and yet without any compromise of divine justice (1 John 1:10).

That's why faith is the starting point of the Christian life, as well as the foundation of true character.

The one true object of genuine saving faith is Christ, as He is revealed in Scripture. Christ Himself said, "Most assuredly, I say to you, he who hears My word and believes in Him who sent Me has everlasting life, and shall not come into judgment, but has passed from death into life" (John 5:24).

> ON THE CROSS GOD TREATED CHRIST AS IF HE HAD COMMITTED ALL THE SINS OF EVERY PERSON WHO WOULD EVER BELIEVE IN HIM, SO THAT HE COULD TREAT THEM AS IF THEY LIVED CHRIST'S PERFECT LIFE.

As we are about to see, faith in Christ is the necessary underpinning for every other virtue of godly character. So before we move on, make sure this most vital prerequisite is settled in your own heart and mind: Do you have authentic faith in Christ?

10

VIRTUE

Although faith is the first and most essential quality of godly character, it is not the only one. Faith simply establishes the necessary framework for every other authentic virtue.

On the one hand, it is crucial to understand faith as something distinct from "good works." As we saw in the previous chapter, faith is the one essential quality without which it is impossible to please God (Hebrews 11:6), while "good works" *never* earn us any merit with God. Much less can our own works purchase (or contribute anything to) atonement, salvation, or forgiveness from our own sin: "For by grace you have been saved through faith, and that not of yourselves; it is the gift of God, not of works, lest anyone should boast" (Ephesians 2:8–9).

On the other hand, it is dangerous to imagine that faith can ever exist in isolation from the good works that are its inevitable fruit, "For we are His workmanship, created in Christ Jesus for good works, which God prepared beforehand that we should walk in them" (Ephesians 2:10). "Faith by itself, if it does not have works, is dead" (James 2:17).

So while we understand and stress that faith in Christ alone is the sole instrument by which we lay hold of forgiveness and full justification, we are not to imagine that true godly character consists in faith by itself apart from other virtues.

The apostle Peter makes this point in 2 Peter 1:5–8, where he urges believers to give all diligence to add other excellent qualities to the faith by which they first laid hold of Christ: "*Giving all diligence, add to your faith virtue*" (v. 5).

> VIRTUE DOESN'T COME
> NATURALLY. IT ISN'T
> SOMETHING THAT HAPPENS
> TO PASSIVE PEOPLE.
> IT REQUIRES DILIGENCE.

"Virtue" in that text is translated from a Greek word that speaks of moral excellence. The word is used only four times in the New Testament. Three of the four usages come from the pen of Peter, and two of them appear in this one verse.

Paul uses the word once, in Philippians 4:8, where it is likewise translated "virtue": "Brethren, whatever things are true, whatever things are noble, whatever things are just, whatever things are pure, whatever things are lovely, whatever things are of good report, if there is any virtue and if there is anything praiseworthy—meditate on these things."

That text essentially equates "virtue" with everything praiseworthy. Moreover, the specific characteristics listed in Philippians 4:8 give us a catalog of qualities that define the multifaceted concept of "virtue": truth, nobility, justice, purity, beauty, and everything good. That would cover everything honorable—from good manners and hospitality in our dealings with others, to righteous thoughts and contentment in the privacy of our own minds.

Add such qualities to your faith, Peter says. Not only that, but be *diligent* to do so. Virtue doesn't come naturally. It isn't something that happens to passive people. It requires diligence.

In other words, while recognizing that we are justified through faith alone apart from any works we do, Peter also recognizes that justifying faith should never remain alone. "Add to your faith," he says.

There is no shortcut to Christlike character. If virtue could be instantly ours through some sort of passive, instantaneous, supernatural faith experience, Peter would have urged us to seek that experience. He doesn't. He commands diligence and describes a process of gradual sanctification whereby we are increasingly conformed to the image of Christ as we exercise diligence in the cultivation of personal virtues.

> THERE IS NO SHORTCUT TO CHRISTLIKE CHARACTER.

That's the way the Christian life is supposed to be, as we are gradually changed "from glory to glory" (2 Corinthians 3:18). Don't be frustrated by the process. Embrace it and be diligent to see it through to the end.

KNOWLEDGE

The next item on Peter's list of moral assets may surprise you: *"Add to your faith virtue, to virtue knowledge"* (2 Peter 1:5). Have you ever thought of *knowledge* as an aspect of godly character? It is.

Now, it's true that knowledge apart from love tends to make a person arrogant (1 Corinthians 8:1). But sinful self-centeredness—not knowledge, per se—is the evil behind that kind of pride.

There is certainly no inherent value or virtue in ignorance. Ignorance is the currency of fools. It is often closely related to sin—both as a cause and as a consequence of evil. Sin makes us spiritually dull, and that is the reason for our frequent lapses into spiritual stupidity. Paul spoke of those who walk "in the futility of their mind, having their understanding darkened, being alienated from the life of God, because of the ignorance that is in them, because of the blindness of their heart" (Ephesians 4:17–18).

> HAVE YOU EVER THOUGHT OF *KNOWLEDGE* AS AN ASPECT OF GODLY CHARACTER? IT IS.

Their sin causes spiritual blindness; the blindness causes a darkening of their understanding; and the ignorance that results breeds even more sin.

You see a clear example of ignorance causing sin and self–righteousness in the case of those described in Romans 10:3, who "being ignorant of God's righteousness, and seeking to establish their own righteousness, have not submitted to the righteousness of God."

Innocence, on the other hand, is indeed a virtue. Paul wrote, "I want you to be wise in what is good, and simple concerning evil" (Romans 16:19). In 1 Corinthians 14:20, he gave a similar admonition: "Do not be children in understanding; however, in malice be babes, but in understanding be mature." Notice how Paul's plea for childlike innocence is actually sandwiched between two commands to be grownups when it comes to understanding the truth.

Knowledge and understanding are the only antidotes to spiritual ignorance. Therefore, says Peter, cultivate knowledge because ignorance actually undermines true character.

This is an admonition well–suited for the shallow and anti–intellectual age in which we live. Lots of people are conditioned to think there's something carnal about the intellect. In the common perception, "spirituality" is supposed to be a state of pseudoconsciousness where the intellect is disengaged and the feelings rule. That is not a biblical perspective.

In fact, Jesus Himself established the virtue of true knowledge when He said, "You shall know the truth, and the truth shall make you free" (John 8:32). Unless we apprehend the truth with our minds, it cannot begin to set us free.

In contrast to the people who disregard knowledge, others in our age believe intellect goes hand in hand with sophistication. They think science and philosophy always trump faith. Some even think modern knowledge has done away with the need for faith. Such people often consider Christians to be unsophisticated or foolish because we profess a real, relevant, living God. But 2 Peter 1:5 admonishes Christians to be exactly what many in the modern world say we're not: knowledgeable.

In Proverbs 1:28–29, God describes the plight of the wicked: "They will seek me diligently, but they will not find me. Because they hated knowledge and did not choose the fear of the LORD." There's nothing "spiritual" about closing one's mind to knowledge. In fact, that is a sure way to incur God's displeasure. But "[Study to show] yourself approved to God, a worker who does not need to be ashamed, rightly dividing the word of truth" (2 Timothy 2:15).

As we have been stressing, the growth process outlined in 2 Peter 1:5–7 must begin with faith. But the rest of Peter's list of virtues should not be considered a chronological checklist—as if we had to finish one item before moving on to the next. Peter isn't suggesting that we first add virtue to our faith, and then when we've finally perfected the issue of personal virtue, we can take up the issue of knowledge. Knowledge must be added as a part of the cultivation of virtue, because knowledge itself is a virtue and one of the essential features of godly character.

Ignorance is the currency

of fools. It is often closely

related to sin—both as a cause

and as a consequence of evil.

Knowledge must be . . . part

of the cultivation of virtue.

12

SELF-CONTROL

"Add . . . to knowledge self-control," Peter says in 2 Peter 1:6. We live, it seems, in a self-indulgent generation, and self-control has become a forgotten character quality. Our grandparents' and great-grandparents' generations were less affluent, and as a result, they knew more about the necessity and the virtue of self-control.

The apostle Paul, hounded by persecution and dogged by hardship throughout his ministry, has much to teach us about self-control. To illustrate the point, Paul uses a metaphor even people in a self-indulgent society can understand: athletics.

He compares life to a race. (This is common imagery in the New Testament, by the way. Other passages that compare life to a foot race include Galatians 5:7; Philippians 2:16; and Hebrews 12:1–2). In 1 Corinthians 9:24 he writes, "Do you not know that those who run in a race all run, but one receives the prize? Run in such a way that you may obtain it."

Every Christian is a competitor, not a spectator, in this race. Life isn't a fun-run, where you participate for the mere pleasure of the social event. It's a real competition, where you have to run to win. The prize is an eternal reward. As Paul said elsewhere, we ought to "press toward the goal for the prize of the upward call of God in Christ Jesus" (Philippians 3:14).

Self-control is absolutely necessary if we are going to achieve victory. "Everyone who competes for the prize is temperate in all things. Now they do it to obtain a perishable crown, but we for an imperishable crown" (1 Corinthians 9:25). In a real race, you can't hope to win if you are forty pounds overweight. Athletes exercise tremendous self-control in order to keep in shape. That's a perfect metaphor for the importance of self-control in the race of life.

The amount of energy an athlete must expend while training to win in competition is staggering. The typical athlete who competes at the Olympic level trains full time for as much as five to ten years before the final competition. He or she learns to endure pain, self-deprivation, and hard work. All of that is involved in the idea of self-control.

> LIFE ISN'T A FUN-RUN. . . . IT'S A REAL COMPETITION, WHERE YOU HAVE TO RUN TO WIN. THE PRIZE IS AN ETERNAL REWARD.

In 1 Corinthians 9:26–27, Paul continues the thought: "Therefore I run thus: not with uncertainty. Thus I fight: not as one who beats the air. But I discipline my body and bring it into subjection." Note that proper self-control involves mastery of one's own body. Legitimate bodily appetites, if not controlled, easily become sin. Gluttony, lust, and laziness are all examples

Self—control also involves the *mind*. If your thought life is not **under control**, evil thinking will quickly erode character, **rob** you of spiritual *victory*, and eventually ruin your life.

of legitimate appetites out of control. All of them destroy character and lead to worse sins.

But self—control also involves the mind. If your thought life is not under control, evil thinking will quickly erode character, rob you of spiritual victory, and eventually ruin your life. "As he thinks in his heart, so is he" (Proverbs 23:7).

In many ways, then, self—control is the key to true character. This is not a virtue you can practice part—time. It's not something you can leave behind when you go on holiday. It is by

> ATHLETES EXERCISE TREMENDOUS SELF—CONTROL IN ORDER TO KEEP IN SHAPE. THAT'S A PERFECT METAPHOR FOR THE IMPORTANCE OF SELF—CONTROL IN THE RACE OF LIFE.

definition a lifelong discipline. Those who fail at this point will ultimately fail spectacularly. Paul understood that. Therefore, he said, "I discipline my body and bring it into subjection, lest, when I have preached to others, I myself should become disqualified" (1 Corinthians 9:27).

Those are sobering words. If no less than the apostle Paul recognized the possibility of being disqualified—set on the shelf, made useless for ministry because of a ruined testimony—then surely we ought to recognize the supreme importance of the same kind of self—control.

13

PERSEVERANCE

Closely aligned with the virtue of self–control is *perseverance*. Peter writes, *"Add . . . to self–control perseverance"* (2 Peter 1:6). As we noted at the conclusion of the previous chapter, there is no such thing as true self–control without perseverance. But perseverance itself is a virtue of the highest order.

In one sense, perseverance is the inevitable result of authentic faith. All genuine Christians persevere in the faith because God Himself keeps them faithful and secure in the faith. In his first epistle, Peter says we "are kept by the power of God through faith for salvation ready to be revealed in the last time" (1 Peter 1:5). Paul told Timothy, "I know whom I have believed and am persuaded that He is able to keep what I have committed to Him until that Day" (2 Timothy 1:12). The apostle John says of those who abandon their profession of faith in Christ, "They went out from us, but they were not of us; for if they had been of us, they would have continued with us; but they went out that they might be made manifest, that none of them were

THE QUEST FOR CHARACTER 63

of us" (1 John 2:19). Authentic faith guarantees perseverance in that sense.

On the other hand, Scripture is full of exhortations urging us to persevere, remain faithful, continue in the pursuit of holiness, abide in Christ, and be diligent to show ourselves approved unto God. Those exhortations remind us that our perseverance, although guaranteed by God in the ultimate sense, nonetheless involves our participation.

Paul encouraged Timothy to persist in the quest for personal character and sound doctrine, knowing that God would thereby bless his ministry: "Take heed to yourself and to the doctrine. Continue in them, for in doing this you will save both yourself and those who hear you" (1 Timothy 4:16). Timothy's perseverance would be the proof that his faith was genuine. Not only that; his perseverance would guarantee that his ministry to others would be fruitful.

PERSEVERANCE IS THE INEVITABLE RESULT OF AUTHENTIC FAITH.

Jesus made perseverance the test of true discipleship: "If you abide in My word, you are My disciples indeed" (John 8:31).

Peter undoubtedly heard that principle from Jesus' own lips numerous times, and he also knew from bitter experience how easy it is to fail despite our best intentions. On the night of Christ's betrayal, Peter succumbed to fear and denied his Lord three times. This happened just after Peter's boast that he would never do such a thing. "Even if all are made to stumble because of You, I will never be made to stumble," he had solemnly promised (Matthew 26:33). Yet when put to the test, Peter failed. He denied Christ in the most egregious fashion, with cursing and swearing (Matthew 26:74).

The experience taught Peter something about perseverance, and the lesson he learned is extremely relevant to this exhortation in 2 Peter 1:6 about self—control and perseverance. Perseverance clearly doesn't mean that we will never fail; it means that when we do fail, we should seek the Lord's promised forgiveness, learn from our failures, and persevere anyway.

The Lord restored Peter, formally commissioning him (three times, in answer to Peter's threefold denial) to be a faithful shepherd to the greater flock (John 21:15—17). And even though that was not Peter's final failure, he kept pressing on. He did not succumb to discouragement; he did not abandon the faith; and he did not repeat the same mistakes over and over. He learned from each mistake and thus drew strength even from his failures.

That's why Peter was eminently qualified to exhort fellow believers to perseverance. He was a living example of the great virtue of spiritual tenacity, and an encouragement to us to persevere in our quest for Christlike character—even when we fail.

Our perseverance, although guaranteed by God in the ultimate sense, nonetheless involves our participation.

14

GODLINESS

Perhaps nothing is more obvious than the truth that Christlike character requires *godliness*. Peter gives this virtue a prominent place in his list of moral qualities that must be added to faith. "*Add . . . to perseverance godliness*" (2 Peter 1:6). The Greek term he employs means "piety," or "reverence." It speaks of conduct, belief, and speech that is harmonious with the character of God and honoring to Him. A derivation of the same Greek word is used in Acts 10:2, where Cornelius is described as a "devout" man.

The term has a more explicitly Godward focus than any of the other words in Peter's list. *Godliness* describes the nature of one's vertical relationship with God. Even in the pagan world of the first century, the term was used commonly to speak of devotion to the gods. So this was a more specific term than *righteousness*, which can also be used to describe one's horizontal relationships with other people.

Authentic godliness is inseparable from the fear of God. Hebrews 12:28–29 says, "Let us have grace, by which we may serve God acceptably with reverence and godly fear. For our God is a consuming fire." Notice that there's a distinction between reverence and godly fear. Occasionally you'll hear someone suggest that the proper fear of God is merely a kind of quiet reverence, or sacred awe—not really anything as unsettling as *fear*. This verse suggests otherwise, reminding us that God's wrath burns against evil. The psalmist was expressing a true dread at the thought of God's vengeance when he wrote, "O LORD, do not rebuke me in Your wrath, nor chasten me in Your hot displeasure!" (Psalm 38:1).

In fact, terror at the thought of God's righteousness is actually a necessary aspect of true reverence and holy awe. Isaiah 8:13 says, "The LORD of hosts, Him you shall hallow; let Him be your fear, and let Him be your dread."

But there's a positive side to godliness also. It involves not only a genuine *fear* of God, but also a deep *passion* for Him. If the fear of God is the necessary foundation of true godliness, here is where the virtue derives

AUTHENTIC GODLINESS IS INSEPARABLE FROM THE FEAR OF GOD.

its real energy. Authentic godliness is an expression of deep love for God.

Someone might object that it is impossible to love someone whom you fear. It's certainly true (according to 1 John 4:18) that love overwhelms every craven variety of fear. Still, fear of God and love for Him are necessary aspects of authentic godliness. In fact, genuine reverence involves both fear and love. This is the very gist of godliness. It is precisely the frame of mind Scripture

demands of us—
fear of God together
with sincere love for Him—
and the result is godly obedience:
"What does the LORD your God require of you, but to fear
the LORD your God, to walk in all His ways and to love Him,
to serve the LORD your God with all your heart and with all
your soul" (Deuteronomy 10:12).

We've seen already that self–control is a vital aspect of good
character, and two chapters ago we observed how Paul illustrated
the need for self–control by pointing to a skilled athlete in
training for a race. As important as physical exercise is, however,
godliness is by far a more crucial matter. Paul himself says so in
1 Timothy 4:8: "Bodily exercise profits a little, but godliness is
profitable for all things, having promise of the life that now is
and of that which is to come."

Think of it: if we would devote the same amount of time and
energy to the exercise of godliness as some people expend each
week at the fitness center, we would profit immeasurably—and
in an eternal sense—from the effort.

That's why, in your lifelong quest for character, you may
never hear a more potent suggestion than these simple words
from the pen of Paul: "Exercise yourself toward godliness"
(1 Timothy 4:7).

[Godliness]

involves not only a genuine

fear of God,

but also a deep

passion for Him.

15

BROTHERLY KINDNESS

Peter's list of virtues is not quite finished: "*Add . . . to godliness brotherly kindness*" (2 Peter 1:7). The Greek expression for "brotherly kindness" is a single word, and it's one I'm sure is already familiar to you: *philadelphia*. The word speaks of fraternal affection.

Now, it would be easy to define this expression too narrowly, as the kindness we show fellow believers. That's certainly a major aspect of what Peter is describing. In fact, love for other Christians is such a natural expression of true saving faith that the apostle John cites it as one of the main evidences of an authentic conversion experience: "We know that we have passed from death to life, because we love the brethren" (1 John 3:14).

But it would be wrong to limit the idea of "brotherly kindness" to the love that is shown among Christians. In the sense Peter is employing the term, "brotherly kindness" is a very broad concept, and it includes the kindness we are to show to our non–Christian neighbors, too.

From the beginning of Scripture to the end, brotherly affection is exalted as one of the noblest of virtues. In the early chapters of Genesis, we have the negative example of Cain, who killed his brother and was condemned for it. Part of his punishment was to become a fugitive and a vagabond (Genesis 4:12), cut off from family and the comforts of home.

The Old Testament law was full of commands instructing the Israelites to show kindness to their own families, neighbors, and even strangers in the land. The model for such kindness was God himself: "The LORD your God is God of gods and Lord of lords, the great God, mighty and awesome, who shows no partiality nor takes a bribe. He administers justice for the fatherless and the widow, and loves the stranger, giving him food and clothing. Therefore love the stranger, for you were strangers in the land of Egypt" (Deuteronomy 10:17–19).

> LOVE FOR OTHER CHRISTIANS IS SUCH A NATURAL EXPRESSION OF TRUE SAVING FAITH THAT THE APOSTLE JOHN CITES IT AS ONE OF THE MAIN EVIDENCES OF AN AUTHENTIC CONVERSION EXPERIENCE.

In the early teaching of the New Testament church there was likewise a frequent stress on the importance of brotherly kindness. Paul, for example, wrote to the Thessalonians: "Concerning brotherly love [*philadelphia*] you have no need that I should write to you, for you yourselves are taught by God to love one another; and indeed you do so toward all the brethren who are in all Macedonia. But we urge you, brethren, that you increase more and more" (1 Thessalonians 4:9–10).

Brotherly kindness is not limited strictly to physical siblings and spiritual brethren. . . .

[The Bible] commands us to show kindness to strangers.

Again, however, brotherly kindness is not limited strictly to physical siblings and spiritual brethren. Just as the Old Testament law included a specific command for showing kindness to strangers, the New Testament likewise commands us to show kindness to strangers. Jesus specifically reiterated the principle of Leviticus 19:18 ("You shall love your neighbor as yourself") and referred to it as the second greatest commandment (Matthew 22:39–40).

In Luke 10:29 an Old Testament legal scholar stood up and tested Jesus with the question: "And who is my neighbor?"

Jesus replied with the parable of the Good Samaritan (vv. 30–37), His now–familiar tale about the man who was beaten and left for dead on the treacherous road from Jerusalem to Jericho. The injured man was passed by a priest and then a Levite before finally being helped by a Samaritan—even though Israelites historically had very low opinions of the Samaritans.

Jesus' point was that whoever comes across your path is your neighbor, and you ought to show brotherly kindness to that person when the opportunity arises. Clearly, "brotherly kindness" is supposed to extend beyond our actual brothers and sisters.

Hebrews 13:1–2 specifically draws the connection between brotherly love and kindness shown to strangers: "Let brotherly love continue. Do not forget to entertain strangers."

16

LOVE

The apostle Peter ends this list of virtues with the greatest of all qualities: *"to brotherly kindness . . . love"* (2 Peter 1:7). We'll have a lot more to say about love in the chapters to come—especially in the closing section of this little book—but Peter introduces the topic for us by making love the capstone of his brief inventory of virtues.

Love is not a separate quality, distinct from the other virtues Peter has already named. Rather, it's best to think of love as a perfect expression of all of them combined. That's clearly how the apostle Paul regards love. After listing a catalog of virtues for the church at Colosse, he writes, "Above all these things put on love, which is the bond of perfection" (Colossians 3:14).

ALL THE VIRTUES ARE INFUSED WITH AND EMPOWERED BY LOVE, AND THAT . . . IS EXACTLY HOW FAITH WORKS.

We'll observe Paul's perspective in detail when we examine the fruit of the Spirit in the next section of this book and then when we unpack Paul's extended description of love from 1 Corinthians 13 in our closing section.

But the common thread running through all these passages is that love is a multifaceted jewel. As a matter of fact, one of the best ways to understand love is to see it as the consummate expression of all God's communicable attributes. That's why when the apostle John wanted to sum up everything that's true about love, he simply wrote, "*God is love*, and he who abides in love abides in God, and God in him" (1 John 4:16, emphasis added). Conversely, "He who does not love does not know God, for God is love" (v. 8).

Consider how love is intimately associated with all the other virtues Peter has been highlighting.

Faith and love are closely linked because, according to the apostle Paul, love is the power that keeps faith from being merely a passive, dormant thing. Faith works through love, he says in Galatians 5:6. The two virtues are such perfect companions that when Paul writes a benediction to the Ephesians, here is what he says: "Peace to the brethren, and *love with faith*, from God the Father and the Lord Jesus Christ" (Ephesians 6:23, emphasis added).

Virtue and love are inseparable, too, because true virtue is motivated by love. Paul summed it up this way: "He who loves another has fulfilled the law. . . . Love is the fulfillment of the law" (Romans 13:8, 10).

James likewise regarded true virtue as the natural expression of love: "If you really fulfill the royal law according to the Scripture, 'You shall love your neighbor as yourself,' you do well" (James 2:8).

Knowledge apart from love is no virtue at all, as we have already learned (1 Corinthians 13:2). Yet knowledge together with love makes a powerful recipe for wisdom. So Paul writes to the Philippians, "This I pray, that your love may abound still more and more in knowledge and all discernment" (Philippians 1:9).

Self–control, perseverance, and *godliness* are simply expressions of true love toward God, in the same way that *brotherly kindness* is an expression of love toward other people.

So all the virtues are infused with and empowered by love, and that, as Paul said in Galatians 5:6, is exactly how faith works.

Peter sums up his list of virtues with this precious promise: "For if these things are yours and abound, you will be neither barren nor unfruitful in the knowledge of our Lord Jesus Christ" (2 Peter 1:8).

Want to make your life count? Cultivate these qualities, Peter says, and you cannot fail.

Love is not a **separate** *quality,* distinct *from the other virtues. . . . [it's] a* **perfect expression** of *all of them combined.*

The Fruit of the Spirit

Galatians 5:22-23

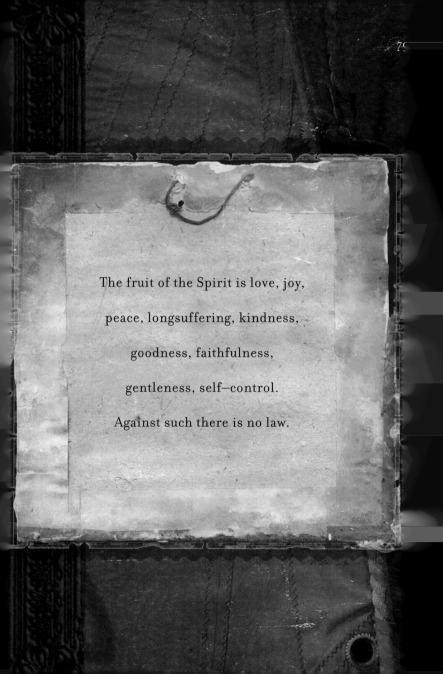

The fruit of the Spirit is love, joy,

peace, longsuffering, kindness,

goodness, faithfulness,

gentleness, self-control.

Against such there is no law.

17

LOVE

In Galatians 5:19–23, the apostle Paul contrasts the works of the flesh with the fruit of the spirit:

Now the works of the flesh are evident, which are: adultery, fornication, uncleanness, lewdness, idolatry, sorcery, hatred, contentions, jealousies, outbursts of wrath, selfish ambitions, dissensions, heresies, envy, murders, drunkenness, revelries, and the like; of which I tell you beforehand, just as I also told you in time past, that those who practice such things will not inherit the kingdom of God. But the fruit of the Spirit is love, joy, peace, longsuffering, kindness, goodness, faithfulness, gentleness, self-control. Against such there is no law.

It's significant that he describes all the vices of fleshly living as "works," and all the virtues of life in the Spirit as "fruit." That reflects one of the fundamental truths of Pauline theology and certainly the central point of his epistle to the Galatians: righteousness cannot be gained by working for it. True virtue is a fruit of the Spirit's life flowing through us.

That reminds us of where we started in this study of character qualities: No one can cultivate genuine virtue apart from saving faith in Christ. These virtues are all fruits of the Spirit's work in and through us.

You cannot manufacture fruit. Fruit grows on its own in the right circumstances and given a suitable environment. You can't get a sweet pear from a bramble bush, and all the factory workers and equipment in the world could never fabricate an orange.

Paul reminds us that real virtue is also a fruit. It cannot be synthesized from other materials. All imitations of the Spirit's fruit are inadequate and ultimately bad–tasting. Such synthetic fruit will be rejected when our works are tested for quality.

> NO ONE CAN CULTIVATE GENUINE VIRTUE APART FROM SAVING FAITH IN CHRIST.

The expression "fruit of the Spirit" reminds us that real virtue is the Holy Spirit's fruit. He is the source and the root of it. It is not something we could ever produce in ourselves.

From the fact that this is the Holy Spirit's fruit, we know it belongs only to those in whom He dwells. Fruit comes from a rooted, abiding, living presence. You'll never get fruit from cut flowers in a vase. You won't see fruit sprout from a fencepost. Fruit is the product of life.

Paul begins his list exactly where Peter ended his—with the grace of *love*: "*The fruit of the Spirit is love.*" Both the noun (*fruit*) and the verb (*is*) are singular, indicating that Paul is not listing nine different fruits of the Spirit. It's one fruit with several characteristics. He begins, naturally, with the single virtue that is most characteristic, most all–inclusive, and the best general term for the fruit he is describing: love.

Don't miss the fact that all the characteristics of spiritual fruit he lists are attitudes as opposed to deeds. Because he is making a point of the contrast between works and fruit, that comes as no surprise.

Still, don't get the idea that Paul is speaking of a love that is passive or inert. Don't imagine that the love of which he speaks is a mere sentiment we "fall" into, or a feeling that comes upon us. Genuine love as Scripture portrays it is a deliberate willingness to serve others and give freely of oneself. Remember that Jesus described the highest expression of love in exactly those terms: "Greater love has no one than this, than to lay down one's life for his friends" (John 15:13).

> GENUINE LOVE . . . IS A DELIBERATE WILLINGNESS TO SERVE OTHERS AND GIVE FREELY OF ONESELF.

Christ Himself is the supreme example of this supreme virtue. He literally laid down His life for others in a self–sacrifice that stands forever as the ultimate example of perfect love.

You cannot manufacture fruit. Fruit grows on its own in the right circumstances and given a suitable environment.

18

JOY

Second in Paul's list of manifestations of the Spirit's fruit is *joy*. Real joy is not a shallow, giddy, fleeting sort of glee, but a deep—down, abiding sense of well—being that stems from the satisfaction a true believer finds in God.

Joy is the natural and expected result of authentic faith in Christ, and it rises above all the trials of life. Peter wrote to people suffering under the harshest kind of persecution, remarking how they rejoiced in the genuineness of their own faith. He reminded them that their faith, "being much more precious than gold that perishes, though it is tested by fire, [would] be found to praise, honor, and glory at the revelation of Jesus Christ, whom having not seen you love. Though now you do not see Him, *yet believing, you rejoice with joy inexpressible and full of glory*" (1 Peter 1:7-8, emphasis added). Such is the reality of Christian joy.

> REAL JOY IS NOT A SHALLOW, GIDDY, FLEETING SORT OF GLEE, BUT A DEEP—DOWN, ABIDING SENSE OF WELL—BEING THAT STEMS FROM THE SATISFACTION A TRUE BELIEVER FINDS IN GOD.

In other words, authentic joy is not the sense of delight we sometimes feel when life deals us favorable circumstances. Real joy may be profound even when our circumstances are most difficult to bear. In fact, as Nehemiah reminded people even in the midst of profound sorrow over their own sin, "The joy of the LORD is your strength" (Nehemiah 8:10).

> REAL JOY MAY BE PROFOUND EVEN WHEN OUR CIRCUMSTANCES ARE MOST DIFFICULT TO BEAR.

Paul was a living example of joy in the midst of trials. Joy is a common theme in all his New Testament epistles even though he often wrote in the midst of his own hardship. As a matter of fact, the only time he *didn't* speak of joy or rejoicing was when he was refuting false doctrine or confronting serious discipline problems in the church.

Everything ultimately seemed to draw Paul's thoughts back to joy and rejoicing. He was full of joy, and he constantly reminded his readers that joy is not only a privilege, but also a *duty*. The second shortest verse in the Bible is the simple command of 1 Thessalonians 5:16: "Rejoice always." In Philippians 4:4 he repeats the same imperative twice for emphasis: "Rejoice in the Lord always. Again I will say, rejoice!"

In Galatians 5, when he lists joy as one of the qualities of the Holy Spirit's fruit, Paul makes it clear that he is not speaking of any natural temperament. Real joy is not merely a personality quirk that belongs to people who are naturally upbeat.

Nor is this kind of joy a response to external stimuli. If Peter can find a reason for joy in the most intense suffering, joy can't be something that rises and falls with our moods. This kind of joy is not a sensual emotion at all. It is a deep gladness that comes from within, and it's prompted partly by the knowledge that God has accepted us in Christ and partly by the delight and satisfaction we find in him.

Within that context there is no limit to the happiness and rejoicing and pleasure we are entitled to enjoy. The great Victorian Baptist preacher Charles Spurgeon had this to say: "You cannot be too happy, brother. Nay, do not suspect yourself of being wrong because you are full of delight. You know that it is said of the divine wisdom, 'Her ways are the ways of pleasantness, and all her paths are peace.' Provided that it is joy in the Lord, you cannot have too much of it."

> JOY IS ONE OF THE TRUE DELIGHTS OF GOD'S KINGDOM, A GREATER BLISS THAN ANY EARTHLY PLEASURE.

Joy is one of the true delights of God's kingdom, a greater bliss than any earthly pleasure. Elsewhere, Paul wrote, "For the kingdom of God is not eating and drinking, but righteousness and peace and joy in the Holy Spirit" (Romans 14:17).

If you are a part of the kingdom, enjoy it!

19

PEACE

If joy is the fruit of an exhilarated heart that finds delight in God, *peace* is the tranquility of a soul who finds rest in Him. Both are products of justifying faith.

As a matter of fact, Paul highlights peace as one of the primary and immediate results of our justification: "Therefore, having been justified by faith, we have peace with God through our Lord Jesus Christ" (Romans 5:1).

Naturally, in this context, as always, Paul names joy as the close partner of such peace: ". . . through whom also we have access by faith into this grace in which we stand, and rejoice in hope of the glory of God" (v. 2).

> PEACE IS THE TRANQUILITY OF A SOUL WHO FINDS REST IN [GOD].

Peace and joy are very similar in that neither is dependent on any external circumstances. True peace rests in the objective reality of our right standing with God and the knowledge that ultimately nothing can snatch us from His loving care.

In fact, the image of this peace is perfectly captured in the pastoral language Jesus used in comparing believers to sheep of whom He is the Great Shepherd: "My sheep hear My voice, and

I know them, and they follow Me. And I give them eternal life, and they shall never perish; neither shall anyone snatch them out of My hand" (John 10:27–28). Peace is His special legacy to His people: "Peace I leave with you, My peace I give to you; not as the world gives do I give to you. Let not your heart be troubled, neither let it be afraid" (John 14:27).

Furthermore, even when trying circumstances *do* come our way (as they inevitably will), we can rest in the knowledge that "all things work together for good to those who love God, to those who are the called according to His purpose" (Romans 8:28). Thus Paul can say, "Be anxious for nothing, but in everything by prayer and supplication, with thanksgiving, let your requests be made known to God; and the peace of God, which surpasses all understanding, will guard your hearts and minds through Christ Jesus" (Philippians 4:6–7).

> PEACE AND JOY ARE VERY SIMILAR IN THAT NEITHER IS DEPENDENT ON ANY EXTERNAL CIRCUMSTANCES.

Remember that the Beatitudes contained a special blessing for peacemakers. When we looked at that passage we observed that in order to be a peacemaker, a person must himself know peace with God. Conversely, a person who knows God's peace will want to spread it. That is the natural effect of peace with God—it is contagious. Peace begets peace. A person who truly knows and loves the peace of God is inevitably a peacemaker.

The power of peace is summed up beautifully in James 3:18: "Now the fruit of righteousness is sown in peace by those who make peace." In other words, peace itself is a potent and productive virtue, reproducing more and more of the fruits of righteousness.

If you ever find yourself weary in the quest for character, here's a wonderful threefold refreshment that will never fail to recharge, renew, and invigorate your soul: *"The fruit of the Spirit is love, joy, peace."*

20

LONGSUFFERING

Longsuffering is one of those biblical words that unfortunately is too often neglected. Here is a character quality that signifies real maturity. The Greek term translated "longsuffering" speaks of endurance despite the taunts and injuries inflicted by others. It contains the ideas of patience, tolerance, forbearance, and restraint—mainly in the midst of painful or irritating trials.

> THE GREEK TERM TRANSLATED "LONGSUFFERING" . . . CONTAINS THE IDEAS OF PATIENCE, TOLERANCE, FORBEARANCE, AND RESTRAINT.

God Himself is slow to anger. Psalm 86 is a hymn about the patience of God, and verse 15 says this: "You, O Lord, are a God full of compassion, and gracious, longsuffering and abundant in mercy and truth." Longsuffering therefore is one of the key traits of God's own character.

We're commanded repeatedly to be patient. One of the key texts on the subject is Colossians 3:12–13, where Paul names longsuffering as part of the proper attire of the new man—the redeemed person in Christ. He writes, "Therefore, as the elect of God, holy and beloved, put on tender mercies, kindness, humility, meekness, longsuffering; bearing with one another, and forgiving one another, if anyone has a complaint against another; even as Christ forgave you, so you also must do."

Notice how many diverse moral qualities are part of this same spirit of patience. Some that we have already discussed include kindness, humility, and meekness. Longsuffering is also closely related to gentleness and self–control, two aspects of the fruit of the Spirit Paul will name

THE SUPREME EXAMPLE OF HUMAN LONGSUFFERING IS CHRIST.

later in this same passage. It's also associated with perseverance, which we talked about in a previous chapter. But longsuffering is a particular *kind* of patient, gentle, persevering self–control that especially comes into play in our dealings with people who deliberately try to provoke us.

Peter had much to say about this virtue in his first epistle. He wrote, "Servants, be submissive to your masters with all fear, not only to the good and gentle, but also to the harsh. For this is commendable, if because of conscience toward God one endures grief, suffering wrongfully. For what credit is it if, when you are beaten for your faults, you take it patiently? But when you do good and suffer, if you take it patiently, this is commendable before God" (1 Peter 2:18–20).

He went on to remind his readers that the supreme example of human longsuffering is Christ, who "when He was reviled, did not revile in return; when He suffered, He did not threaten, but committed Himself to Him who judges righteously" (v. 23).

LONGSUFFERING IS A PARTICULAR *kind* OF PATIENT, GENTLE, PERSEVERING SELF—CONTROL THAT ESPECIALLY COMES INTO PLAY IN OUR DEALINGS WITH PEOPLE WHO DELIBERATELY TRY TO PROVOKE US.

That is the epitome of longsuffering. You can see why this trait is a particular emblem of spiritual maturity. Such patient longsuffering comes naturally to no one.

At this point, if you feel as if the quest for character has brought you into rarefied atmosphere, you're getting the point. Hang on. There's more yet to come.

21

KINDNESS

The next characteristic of spiritual fruit in Galatians 5:22 is *kindness*. Paul uses a completely different Greek word from the one translated "brotherly kindness" in 2 Peter 1. The word Peter uses describes an attitude of fraternal affection; Paul uses an unrelated Greek expression that emphasizes tender concern, gentleness, and consideration for others.

Like their English counterparts, all the New Testament words describing kindness, meekness, gentleness, goodness, love, and similar qualities include a lot of overlapping ideas. Paul's purpose is not to establish distinct categories for us to think about separately. He is deliberately employing a variety of similar terms and close synonyms to help us get the big picture more clearly. Remember, he is showing several facets of the fruit of the Holy Spirit—which is a single fruit with manifold expressions. And he's simply giving us the flavor of it with all these related concepts.

Like all the virtues we have discussed, the characteristics of the Holy Spirit's fruit are interdependent qualities—and at points almost indistinguishable from one another. That is deliberate. Godly character is not the sum of many disparate attributes. It is the single quality of *Christlikeness*. Try to isolate these moral qualities from one another and you destroy them all.

Nonetheless, each word has a layer of significance that helps round out the concept of godly character in all its nuances.

The idea of gentleness and tenderness involved in this expression has nothing to do with weakness or feebleness. Tenderheartedness is not the same as faintheartedness. True kindness is actually a gracious *strength*. It presupposes a steadfast tenacity that sees a relationship through trials and hardship. This is the kindness that offers help and support in times of need. In fact, the Greek word is derived from an expression that speaks of helpfulness.

The same Greek word is often translated "goodness." In fact, the word is used often in the New Testament to speak of God's goodness to unbelievers. As such, it is a reminder that we are commanded to do good even to those who hate us and persecute us (Matthew 5:44).

It's also one more reminder that there is a gentle side to authentic character. Paul says that those who lack this quality are not fit to be leaders in the church, because "a servant of the Lord must not quarrel but be gentle to all, able to teach, patient, in humility correcting those who are in opposition, if God perhaps will grant them repentance, so that they may know the truth" (2 Timothy 2:24–25).

Godly character is not the sum of many disparate attributes. It is the single quality of Christlikeness.

Tenderheartedness is not the same as faintheartedness. True kindness is actually a gracious strength. It presupposes a steadfast tenacity that sees a relationship through trials and hardship.

GOODNESS

The next feature of the fruit of the Spirit is a generic term for *goodness*. Like its English counterpart, the Greek expression Paul employs signifies moral excellence in general—virtue, beneficence, uprightness, and everything similar. The term is no more specific in the original text than it is in the modern translations. It speaks of decency and good character in general.

It's a completely different word from the one Peter used in 2 Peter 1:5, when he wrote, "add to your faith *virtue*"—but the two words are nonetheless close synonyms. This one is the same word Paul employed when he wrote to the church at Rome, "I myself am confident concerning you, my brethren, that you also are full of *goodness*, filled with all knowledge, able also to admonish one another" (Romans 15:14). He used the word again in Ephesians 5, as part of a shorthand description of the fruit of the Spirit: "The fruit of the Spirit is in all goodness, righteousness, and truth" (Ephesians 5:9).

So this is essentially an all-purpose description of virtue in general. It means goodness as opposed to badness. It also implies the idea of *active* goodness—an attitude that seeks to *do* good, as opposed to just being passively benign and agreeable.

This same word is used to describe the goodness of God in
2 Thessalonians 1:11: "Therefore we also pray always for you that
our God would count you worthy of this calling, and fulfill all the
good pleasure of His *goodness* and the work of faith with power."
In that instance, divine goodness
is pictured as an attribute
whereby God takes pleasure in
the good works of His people,
especially toward one another.

As we have seen repeatedly,
the Christian's goodness toward
others is not supposed to be
strictly limited to fellow
believers only. But it certainly is
appropriate to keep it focused
primarily in that direction. To that end Paul writes, "As we have
opportunity, let us do good to all, especially to those who are of
the household of faith" (Galatians 6:10).

That exhortation is immediately preceded by these words of
encouragement: "And let us not grow weary while doing good,
for in due season we shall reap if we do not lose heart" (v. 9).

> THE CHRISTIAN'S
> GOODNESS TOWARD OTHERS
> IS NOT SUPPOSED TO BE
> STRICTLY LIMITED TO
> FELLOW BELIEVERS ONLY.
> BUT IT CERTAINLY IS
> APPROPRIATE TO KEEP IT
> FOCUSED PRIMARILY IN
> THAT DIRECTION.

23

FAITHFULNESS

"The fruit of the Spirit is . . . *faithfulness*." In Galatians 5:22 the King James Version simply says "faith," because the Greek word is actually the same for both ideas. That's fitting, because "faith" and "faithfulness" are so closely related that sometimes they may even appear inseparable. Yet it's important to distinguish the concepts.

Faith, of course, is a belief in the truth of something. Authentic faith is the work of the Holy Spirit in a person's heart; it is not something the carnal heart can conjure up out of its own free will. "Because the carnal mind is enmity against God; for it is not subject to the law of God, nor indeed can be. So then, those who are in the flesh cannot please God" (Romans 8:7–8).

Genuine saving faith is a wholehearted submission to the simple truth of the gospel. It involves personal trust in Christ as Lord and Savior, as well as a conviction that the truth claims of the gospel are reliable.

Thus faith has built right into it a principle that engenders the quality of *faithfulness*—which is a steadfast devotion to the truth. Faith and faithfulness must be distinguished for good reason—because faith in Christ (simple trust in Him as Lord and Savior) is the only instrument of our justification—completely apart from works of any kind. Paul stresses this truth in Galatians 2:16: "Knowing that a man is not justified by the works of the law but by faith in Jesus Christ, even we have believed in Christ Jesus, that we might be justified by faith in Christ and not by the works of the law; for by the works of the law no flesh shall be justified."

WE ARE JUSTIFIED BY *faith*, NOT *faithfulness*, AND IT'S VITAL TO UNDERSTAND THE DISTINCTION.

In other words, we are justified by *faith*, not *faithfulness*, and it's vital to understand the distinction.

Still, faithfulness is impossible apart from saving faith, and true saving faith comes with a built-in spirit that produces long-term faithfulness. You'll recall when we looked at the idea of perseverance in 2 Peter 1:6, we saw that true faith *always* perseveres. Here is why: genuine faith always begets faithfulness. And both are the fruit of the Holy Spirit's work in our hearts.

The quality and constancy of our faithfulness may vary in lesser or greater degrees from time to time. Like Peter, we are prone to failure. Before Peter ever denied Christ, you may recall, Jesus told him, "Satan has asked for you, that he may sift you as wheat. But I have prayed for you, that your faith should not fail" (Luke 22:31–32). And that prayer was answered. Peter's faith remained steadfast even though he himself failed badly. In the ultimate sense, he kept the faith. He emerged from the trial badly bruised, but still faithful and even more deeply devoted to Christ.

GENUINE FAITH ALWAYS BEGETS FAITHFULNESS. AND BOTH ARE THE FRUIT OF THE HOLY SPIRIT'S WORK IN OUR HEARTS.

God Himself is always unwaveringly faithful, according to Scripture: "If we are faithless, He remains faithful; He cannot deny Himself" (2 Timothy 2:13).

24

GENTLENESS

Here's a concept closely related to the idea of meekness, which we discussed back in chapter 3. *Gentleness*. The Greek expression Paul uses is different from the word translated "meek" in the Beatitudes, but the idea is very similar. This word describes a particular kind of gentle meekness that enables us to respond patiently to the faults of others as well as their offenses against us.

The word is uniquely Pauline. No other writer in Scripture employs it, but Paul uses it nine times throughout his epistles. We first encounter the word in 1 Corinthians 4. In that context, Paul is responding to some critics in the church who seemed to be deliberately stirring strife against him. He had sent Timothy as his representative to deal with the conflict, but some of Paul's detractors used even that as a reason to criticize, complaining because Paul himself had not come. He replies, "I will come to you shortly, if the Lord wills. . . . What do you want? Shall I come to you with a rod, or in love and a spirit of *gentleness*?" (1 Corinthians 4:19–21, emphasis added).

Elsewhere, he uses the word again to describe how Christians ought to deal with sin when they see it in fellow

Gentleness . . . describes a particular kind of gentle meekness that enables us to respond patiently to the faults of others as well as their offenses against us.

Gentleness is part of the essential wardrobe of the new man.

believers: "Brethren, if a man is overtaken in any trespass, you who are spiritual restore such a one in a spirit of *gentleness*, considering yourself lest you also be tempted" (Galatians 6:1, emphasis added).

In 2 Timothy 2:24–25, the same word is translated "humility," but what Paul describes is the very same concept as he suggests that it ought to characterize the way Christian leaders deal with people under their oversight: "And a servant of the Lord must not quarrel but be gentle to all, able to teach, patient, in *humility* correcting those who are in opposition, if God perhaps will grant them repentance, so that they may know the truth" (emphasis added).

So what this term describes is a tender, considerate, patient, humble spirit of compassion when dealing with others' offenses and failures. Jesus Himself epitomized this quality. Paul appealed to that very trait in yet another plea to his critics in Corinth. He wrote, "Now I, Paul, myself am pleading with you by the meekness and gentleness of Christ . . ." (2 Corinthians 10:1).

It might not be our first inclination to respond to others' faults with such gentle meekness, but it is nearly always the best and most effective way to respond. Therefore, Paul says, we should wear gentleness like a fine garment. Together with other traits we have already considered, such as longsuffering and kindness, gentleness is part of the essential wardrobe of the new man (Colossians 3:12–13).

SELF-CONTROL

Of course, self-control is one of the qualities Peter listed as traits to be added to faith, and we already looked at it in chapter 12 of this book. But Paul likewise names it in Galatians 5 as one of the characteristics of the Holy Spirit's fruit, and he employs the very same Greek word Peter used. So we return to the concept for another look.

Perhaps you've noticed that all the virtues we have discussed imply the necessity of self-control. Gentleness, for example, requires a measure of godly restraint. The person who lacks gentleness also lacks self-control. So again we discover that all these virtues are inter-woven. In practical terms, any one of them presupposes all the others.

Self-control, you'll recall, is the exercise of godly restraint upon our human appetites and passions. This quality is practically the lifeblood of virtue itself—so that a person of true character is most easily distinguished by his or her extraordinary self-control. In the

development of Christlike character qualities, here is a trait
to which we ought to give a significant amount of energy and
attention.

Solomon, who was by no means a master of self—control
himself, nonetheless saw the importance of this trait. He wrote,
"Whoever has no rule over his own spirit is like a city broken
down, without walls" (Proverbs 25:28). The person who lacks
self—control is naturally defenseless against temptation. Without
self—control, therefore, no other virtue will endure for long.

Solomon may have lacked self—control, but he was not
lacking in wisdom (1 Kings 10:23). He understood what it takes
to have true self—control: "Keep your heart with all diligence,
for out of it spring the issues
of life" (Proverbs 4:23).
In other words, your heart
is the reservoir of life. What
comes out of it can either help
you grow strong or defile you.

> ALL THE VIRTUES . . .
> IMPLY THE NECESSITY
> OF SELF—CONTROL.

Jesus taught this same truth: "What comes out of a man,
that defiles a man. For from within, out of the heart of men,
proceed evil thoughts, adulteries, fornications, murders, thefts,
covetousness, wickedness, deceit, lewdness, an evil eye, blasphemy,
pride, foolishness. All these evil things come from within and
defile a man" (Mark 7:20—23).

If you truly want to exercise self—control, you have to start
by controlling your own thoughts. An evil thought—life will erode
character more quickly and more certainly than any other influence,

because the evil things that come from our own hearts are the things that defile us the most.

This is an especially vital lesson for those of us living in the Internet generation. We are daily assaulted with images and advertising deliberately designed to appeal to the lust of the flesh, the lust of the eyes, and sinful human pride (1 John 2:16)— and the only way to remain pure in the midst of such an assault is by exercising careful self–control over our thought life.

The fact that you're reading a book like this suggests that you see the importance of guarding your heart. Let me encourage you in that pursuit with the message of Romans 13:14, which offers the best advice I know for achieving self–control: "Put on the Lord Jesus Christ, and make no provision for the flesh, to fulfill its lusts."

If you truly want to exercise self—control, you have to start by controlling your own thoughts.

THE TRIUMPH OF LOVE

1 CORINTHIANS 13:4-8

Love suffers long and is kind; love does

not envy; love does not parade itself,

is not puffed up; does not behave rudely,

does not seek its own, is not provoked,

thinks no evil; does not rejoice in

iniquity, but rejoices in the truth;

bears all things, believes all things,

hopes all things, endures all things.

Love never fails.

26

LOVE

The sum of all other virtues is love. Scripture repeatedly makes that clear by saying that the whole law is fulfilled in this one word (Galatians 5:14). Jesus said all the law and the prophets hang on two commandments about love: love God, and love your neighbor (Matthew 22:37–40). To the Romans, Paul wrote:

> *Owe no one anything except to love one another,*
> *for he who loves another has fulfilled the law.*
> *For the commandments, "You shall not commit*
> *adultery," "You shall not murder," "You shall not*
> *steal," "You shall not bear false witness,"*
> *"You shall not covet," and if there is any other*
> *commandment, are all summed up in this saying,*
> *namely, "You shall love your neighbor as yourself."*
> *Love does no harm to a neighbor; therefore love*
> *is the fulfillment of the law.*
>
> —ROMANS 38:8–10

This, then, is where the quest for character inevitably brings us, and it's fitting that we close the book with miniature chapters examining one by one all the characteristics of love given in the apostle Paul's poetic description of love in 1 Corinthians 13. Some of these may feel like familiar ground, but if you really want to grasp the very essence of Christlike character, it is vital to see all virtues' relationship to love.

Without love, Paul says, all other virtues are mere pretense. He uses vivid language to make the point:

> *Though I speak with the tongues of men and of angels, but have not love, I have become sounding brass or a clanging cymbal. And though I have the gift of prophecy, and understand all mysteries and all knowledge, and though I have all faith, so that I could remove mountains, but have not love, I am nothing. And though I bestow all my goods to feed the poor, and though I give my body to be burned, but have not love, it profits me nothing.*

—1 CORINTHIANS 13:1–3

Without *love*

. . . all other

virtues are mere

pretense.

That surely places the importance of love in proper context. Without love, whatever we say is just so much noise. Without love, whatever other gifts we may have amount to nothing. Without love, all good works are without merit.

> THE SUM OF ALL OTHER VIRTUES IS LOVE.

From there, the apostle gives us a detailed look at the nuances of authentic love. It is as if he shined love through a prism in order to expose the spectrum of virtues contained in love. Then he points out some of the outstanding hues.

The result is quite a list, and it helps to round out our understanding of true, Christlike character.

27

SUFFERS LONG

Longsuffering is the virtue we examined in chapter 20, so this is indeed familiar ground. Here, Paul considers longsuffering as an expression of love.

He uses the verb form of the very same noun he had employed for "longsuffering" in Galatians 5:22. It's from a compound Greek expression that literally means "long–tempered." So if you think of what it means to be short–tempered, and then imagine the exact opposite, you have the concept.

Love's longsuffering is expressed in a patient willingness to bear any inconvenience or sacrifice for the sake of our loved one without becoming upset or angry. One of the greatest preachers of the early church, Chrysostom, said this expression describes someone who is wronged and who has the power to avenge himself—but never does it.

Love's *longsuffering* is expressed in a patient *willingness* to bear any inconvenience or sacrifice *for the sake* of our *loved one* without becoming upset or angry.

28

IS KIND

The idea of love's *kindness* also contains an echo of the fruit of the Spirit, and it brings us back to a virtue we have considered in various ways before.

Here's a helpful way to see what Paul is saying: Kindness is the perfect counterpart and the exact mirror image of patience. Whereas patience is a willingness to *take* anything from those whom we love, kindness, by contrast, is a willingness to *give* of every good thing—even to our enemies. That sort of give-and-take benevolence is the epitome of true love.

Furthermore, kindness is an *active* goodwill. It's not merely a "feeling" of generosity; it is a dynamic, sacrificial, unselfish liberality that actually gives of oneself to others.

The best barometer of Christian kindness (and the true test of all love's qualities) is what takes place in the context of home and family—how we treat those closest to us. The husband with true character will be especially kind to his own wife and children. Brothers and sisters show true character by being kind to one another and to their parents. If you're not kind to those in the circle of your own home, you aren't being a good model of the excellent character of love.

Kindness is an

ACTIVE goodwill.

True love is

delighted,

never grudging, when

the object of love

receives blessing.

29

Love DOES NOT ENVY

Authentic love also can be identified by what it's not. Paul lists eight such attributes, starting with the fact that love is *not* envious.

The Greek word for "envy" has the same root as the English word "zeal." It describes a powerful desire—in this case, a sinful and selfish desire.

Don't confuse envy with righteous jealousy. Scripture says, "The Lord, whose name is Jealous, is a jealous God" (Exodus 34:14). That kind of jealousy is a holy indignation in the presence of faithlessness. The jealousy of envy is something completely different. It is a selfish and sinful resentment when others are blessed.

True love is delighted, never grudging, when the object of love receives blessing. James says envy is the root of all kinds of bitterness: "Where envy and self–seeking exist, confusion and every evil thing are there" (James 3:16).

Love prompts the exact opposite response, rejoicing in the success and blessing of others. The opposite of envy is self–sacrifice for the sake of the one whom we love, and Jesus Himself said that is the mark of the highest kind of love (John 15:13).

30

DOES NOT PARADE ITSELF

"Love does not parade itself," Paul says (1 Corinthians 13:4). In other words, love is never ostentatious or vainglorious. Paul employs a unique word that speaks of boasting.

If envy is resentment over the blessings of others, boasting is the sin of trying to make others envious of us. Envy puts others down; boasting is an attempt to elevate self.

It's fitting that Paul wrote these words to the church at Corinth, because bragging was their besetting sin. That church was filled with spiritual showoffs. Some boasted that they were followers of this or that teacher ("I am of Paul," or "I am of Apollos," or "I am of Cephas," or "I am of Christ"—1 Corinthians 1:12). Others were vying for recognition in the exercise of their spiritual gifts. In fact, 1 Corinthians 12 was written to address this sin. Still others were even treating the Lord's Table as a competition to see who could be served first (1 Corinthians 11:21).

In answer to all those evils, Paul exalted the glory of love, and this is one of his key points: Authentic love is incompatible with a self–aggrandizing love for public recognition.

Envy puts others down; boasting is an attempt to elevate self.

31

Love IS NOT PUFFED UP

Continuing with a similar idea, Paul writes, "Love . . . is not puffed up" (1 Corinthians 13:4). The same expression is found seven times in the New Testament. Five of those times are in 1 Corinthians and one is in Colossians 2:18. It's from a Greek expression that literally means "inflated," or "pumped full of air." It is a picturesque, fitting description for a particularly sinister kind of arrogance or bigheadedness.

True love is bighearted but never bigheaded. Arrogance is destructive of love because it is so inherently self–centered. Love and pride are virtual opposites.

Earlier in the epistle, Paul reminded the Corinthians that they had no reason for arrogance. He asked them a series of questions designed to make them contemplate the utter

TRUE LOVE IS BIGHEARTED BUT NEVER BIGHEADED.

inappropriateness of all human pride: "Who makes you differ from another? And what do you have that you did not receive? Now if you did indeed receive it, why do you boast as if you had not received it?" (4:7).

In other words, since we owe everything good about us solely to the gracious work of God, there's no reason for any Christian ever to be puffed up. Genuine love maintains that perspective and therefore lavishes honor and respect on others, not self.

Bad manners

reflect a lack of

grace and love.

32

DOES NOT BEHAVE RUDELY

Here's an aspect of love your mother probably tried to teach you even when you were a child: "Love . . . does not behave rudely" (1 Corinthians 13:5). Love is not ill-mannered and inconsiderate.

If arrogance is an evil craving for honor of oneself, the epitome of bad manners is a failure to show proper honor to others. This is sometimes a sin of omission, sometimes a sin of commission. Either way, it stems from a loveless fixation with oneself.

Here, too, the apostle Paul seems to mention this aspect of love as a particular failing of the church in Corinth. Not only were the Corinthians behaving in an unseemly manner at the Lord's Table (1 Corinthians 11:21), but their worship services were chaotic because everyone was talking at the same time (14:23). Paul gave them this command as a corrective: "Let all things be done decently and in order" (v. 40).

Bad manners reflect a lack of grace and love. Common courtesy is a far more important character quality than most people realize.

33

DOES NOT SEEK ITS OWN

Notice how many of love's attributes have to do with selflessness. Selflessness in a real sense is the very pinnacle of love. "Love . . . does not seek its own" (1 Corinthians 13:5).

In this same epistle to the Corinthians, Paul had earlier written, "Let no one seek his own, but each one the other's well-being" (10:24). He compared the church to a body, with different members—not all hands or eyes, but each essential in its own way, and he pleaded with the Corinthians "that there should be no schism in the body, but that the members should have the same care for one another" (12:25).

Likewise, he wrote to the church at Philippi, "Let nothing be done through selfish ambition or conceit, but in lowliness of mind let each esteem others better than himself. Let each of you look out not only for his own interests, but also for the interests of others" (Philippians 2:3–4).

Again, selfless sacrifice and a concern for the needs of others is the very essence of authentic love. The apostle John wrote, "Whoever has this world's goods, and sees his brother in need, and shuts up his heart from him, how does the love of God abide in him?" (1 John 3:17).

Selfless **sacrifice**

and a **concern** *for*

the needs of others is

the very **essence**

of authentic **love.**

34

Love IS NOT PROVOKED

Love is not swift to take personal offense. James 1:19–20 contains an exhortation about this very issue: "Let every man be swift to hear, slow to speak, slow to wrath; for the wrath of man does not produce the righteousness of God." A bad temper is extremely destructive. Outbursts of anger can be like nuclear bombs; even if short and sudden, they can do tremendous damage. Such anger is rooted in a deficient love, and the conscious, deliberate cultivation of Christlike love is the only cure.

> A BAD TEMPER . . . IS ROOTED IN A DEFICIENT LOVE, AND THE CONSCIOUS, DELIBERATE CULTIVATION OF CHRISTLIKE LOVE IS THE ONLY CURE.

There is no more important element in all the qualities of Christlike character. Remember that when Jesus was reviled, He did not strike back (1 Peter 2:23). The only incidents in the Gospels where Christ ever showed anger were expressions of righteous indignation when God's glory was being openly trampled by unscrupulous men (Mark 3:5; 11:15–17; John 2:15–17). He was always slow to anger. Indeed, even that is an expression of His deity (Psalm 145:8). Never do we see a display of human irritability from Christ.

Scripture says, "A quick–tempered man acts foolishly" (Proverbs 14:17), and "He who is slow to wrath has great understanding, but he who is impulsive exalts folly" (v. 29).

One of the best ways to build strength of character and cultivate love is by learning to control your temper. As Solomon wrote, "He who is slow to anger is better than the mighty, and he who rules his spirit than he who takes a city" (Proverbs 16:32).

35

THINKS NO EVIL

You have surely seen the famous illustration of three monkeys with their hands respectively covering eyes, ears, and mouth: "See no evil. Hear no evil. Speak no evil." I've always thought there should be a fourth monkey, perhaps with his hands covering his forehead, signifying this idea: "Think no evil." In fact, the idea of thinking no evil encompasses the other three.

"Love . . . thinks no evil," Paul writes (1 Corinthians 13:5). And he uses a particular Greek expression for the word "think." It's an accounting term meaning "reckon." It is a word that speaks of recordkeeping and the tabulation of accounts. So the idea here is very specific. This has little to do with thinking about evil things in general. It's about imputing evil motives to others and keeping a tally of wrongs suffered. To borrow the language of another translation, love "does not take into account a wrong suffered" (NASB).

In other words, love has a short memory when it comes to offenses and a positive outlook in the assumptions it makes. Love is always eager to believe the best.

This sort of optimism is a fine character quality, reflecting a spirit of eager forgiveness and trust. It is one of the most beautiful aspects of love, and a mirror of the way God loves us, not reckoning our trespasses against us (Romans 4:8; 2 Corinthians 5:19).

LOVE IS ALWAYS EAGER TO BELIEVE THE BEST.

36

DOES NOT REJOICE
IN INIQUITY

Love finds no satisfaction in sin—whether our own sin or the sins of others. To rejoice in iniquity is to turn virtue and truth on their heads. That violates the spirit of Isaiah 5:20: "woe to those who call evil good, and good evil; who put darkness for light, and light for darkness; who put bitter for sweet, and sweet for bitter!"

We live in a culture that glorifies iniquity. Today's popular entertainment and music reflect this, and that means authentic love requires that we stand apart from the world. In other words, there is an all–too–common kind of love that is utterly incompatible with the true love of God: "If anyone loves the world, the love of the Father is not in him" (1 John 2:15).

> LOVE FINDS NO SATISFACTION IN SIN—WHETHER OUR OWN SIN OR THE SINS OF OTHERS.

If you genuinely love someone, you cannot rejoice when that person sins. Still less would you deliberately want to cause a loved one to stumble. Thus, authentic love goes out of its way not to drag the ones we love into sin or temptation.

Often we hear people try to justify a sin like fornication by using "love" as an excuse: "We just fell in love and couldn't resist." That's not authentic love. Real love does not rejoice in iniquity.

The purity of love is one of the things that makes it the highest of virtues. If you ever imagine that "love" is an excuse for wrongdoing, you need to examine the matter more closely. Real love never delights in evil.

37

REJOICES IN THE TRUTH

On the other hand, authentic love "rejoices in the truth" (1 Corinthians 13:6). With this phrase, Paul begins listing five more positives aspects of love.

At first glance, the contrast may seem slightly askew. Shouldn't the verse say, "does not rejoice in iniquity, but rejoices in *righteousness*"?

"Truth" in this context is actually a comprehensive term that includes all aspects of righteousness. It's not just propositional truth (sound doctrine and factual truth), although it *includes* that. But here truth is a broad concept that embraces righteous thinking, holy living, the revealed truth of Scripture, and even Christ, who is the embodiment of truth (John 14:6).

REAL LOVE SEEKS TO EXALT THE TRUTH— *especially* THE REVEALED TRUTH OF SCRIPTURE.

This clearly eliminates the idea of "love" as something that ignores false teaching, overlooks errors in doctrine, and neglects the objective truth of Scripture while defining what's "good" only in terms of broad, community-based moral values.

Real love seeks to exalt the truth—*especially* the revealed truth of Scripture, which is the only truth that can set people free from their sin (John 8:32).

This is an important mark of genuinely Christlike character—especially in an age when truth is often contrasted with love, as if the two virtues were mutually exclusive. Real love is utterly inconsistent with deliberate compromise of the truth.

38

BEARS ALL THINGS

The final four characteristics of love listed in 1 Corinthians 13 are stated in the form of hyperbole—a deliberate exaggeration to make a point powerfully. They are not to be interpreted with wooden, literal exactitude. Clearly, love does not bear, believe, hope, and endure *all* things without exception, because it's no virtue to accept a lie.

Nonetheless, this short series employs overstatement for a good reason: to stress the extremes to which love will go in its optimism and willingness to sacrifice.

ALTHOUGH LOVE DOES NOT COUNTENANCE OR REJOICE IN SIN, LOVE DOES MAKE US EAGER TO PROTECT THE SINNER AND UPHOLD MERCY AND COMPASSION.

Love "bears all things," the apostle says first (v. 7). He employs a word that means both "cover with silence" and "endure." The concept covers a lot of ground. It rules out the idea of gossiping about our exposing another person's wrongdoing. It also rules out the practice of tale—bearing and listening to gossip.

It furthermore conveys the idea (again) of silently enduring wrongs suffered. This is the patient endurance of one who bears a personal hurt rather than stir further strife. It's the same attitude Paul commended in 1 Corinthians 6:7, when he said it is better to accept a wrong and allow yourself to be cheated than to go to court against a fellow believer.

In other words, although love does not countenance or rejoice in sin, love does make us eager to protect the sinner and uphold mercy and compassion. In the words of the sage, "Hatred stirs up strife, but love covers all sins" (Proverbs 10:12).

Peter wrote about this same virtue in 1 Peter 4:8, and quoted from that very Proverb when he said, "Above all things have fervent love for one another, for 'love will cover a multitude of sins.'"

39

BELIEVES ALL THINGS

Love not only bears all things, it *believes* all things, too. Again, this is not to suggest that love is literally gullible. But it means authentic love is not suspicious or cynical. When it covers a wrong, it also believes the best and wishes for the best outcome for the wrongdoer.

Especially in cases in which we really cannot know the truth about a person's guilt or motives, authentic love is prone to believe the best, not the worst. Love assumes the best motives. Love assumes innocence until guilt is proven. Love engenders trust.

> LOVE ASSUMES THE BEST MOTIVES. LOVE ASSUMES INNOCENCE UNTIL GUILT IS PROVEN. LOVE ENGENDERS TRUST.

These are fine qualities and are all too rare in an increasingly cynical world. One of the sins of Job's counselors was that they were too willing to believe the worst about him rather than the best. Many of the things they told him were true enough, but they did not apply to Job's case. Because his friends imagined the worst, they did not understand what was happening to Job, and the Lord rebuked them severely for it.

Love is supposed to be a safe haven of trust. And even when that trust is broken, love's first response is a desire to heal and restore. "Brethren, if a man is overtaken in any trespass, you who are spiritual restore such a one in a spirit of gentleness, considering yourself lest you also be tempted. Bear one another's burdens, and so fulfill the law of Christ" (Galatians 6:1–2).

Love *refuses*

to see *failure*

as final.

40

HOPES ALL THINGS

Even when love's trust is shattered, love still hopes. If love's faith is betrayed, it still clings to hope. Love refuses to see failure as final.

We often employ the word *hope* to express a longing for something for which there is little or no chance. *Hope* in biblical terms expresses something completely different. It is an earnest expectation. It contains the ideas of confidence, conviction, and anticipation.

Paul is pointing out that true love's hopefulness is difficult to quench. It starts by believing the best. It endures despite setbacks. And even in the face of the worst trials, true love remains expectant.

Paul deliberately portrays love in terms of undying, indefatigable optimism. Again, such optimism is not a weakness of character; it is a great strength, as well as a great source of strength to those who have it.

41

LOVE
ENDURES ALL THINGS AND NEVER FAILS

Finally, Paul writes, "Love…endures all things" (1 Corinthians 13:7). He employs a Greek military term that describes the holding of a position at all costs.

Love holds fast to its object. It withstands every storm and every type of opposition. It refuses to lose faith, falter in its perseverance, or stop hoping. Thus it never stops loving.

> LOVE . . . WITHSTANDS EVERY STORM AND EVERY TYPE OF OPPOSITION. IT REFUSES TO LOSE FAITH, FALTER IN ITS PERSEVERANCE, OR STOP HOPING. THUS IT NEVER STOPS LOVING.

Love bears what may seem unbearable. After that, it believes the seemingly unbelievable. After that, it hopes against hope. And even after that, it endures.

There is no "after" after endurance, because endurance is the climax of love.

Indeed, love's permanence is what makes it the greatest of virtues. At the end of 1 Corinthians 13, Paul writes, "And now abide faith, hope, love, these three; but the greatest of these is love" (v. 13).

At the moment, we walk by faith, not by sight (2 Corinthians 5:7). We live by hope, "but hope that is seen is not hope; for why does one still hope for what he sees?" (Romans 8:24).

One day, faith will give way to perfect understanding, and hope will be swallowed up by perfect sight. "For now we see in a mirror, dimly, but then face to face. Now I know in part, but then I shall know just as I also am known" (1 Corinthians 13:12).

Then love will stand as the only eternal virtue, because "Love never fails" (v. 8).

That is why love is the very pinnacle and the highest aspiration in the quest for character. For in the perfection of love, we meet the very essence of true Christlikeness.

> IN THE PERFECTION OF LOVE, WE MEET THE VERY ESSENCE OF TRUE CHRISTLIKENESS.

Beloved, now we are children of God; and it has not yet been revealed what we shall be, but we know that when He is revealed, we shall be like Him, for we shall see Him as He is (1 John 3:2).

ABOUT THE AUTHOR
FOR MORE INFO

Grace to You is the Bible-teaching media ministry of John MacArthur. In addition to producing the worldwide *Grace to You* and *Grace to You Weekend* radio broadcasts, the ministry distributes more than fifty books by John MacArthur and has produced more than fourteen million audio messages since 1969.

For more details about John MacArthur and all his Bible-teaching resources, contact Grace to You at 800-55-GRACE (800-554-7223) or www.gty.org.